GYPSIES OF IRAQ:

Cultural Characteristics, Social Adaptation and Integration

Hamied Al-Hashimi

Translated by: Hassan Hadi
Foreword by: Sarah Edgcumbe

Designed and printed by Dolman Scott Ltd

DolmanScott
www.dolmanscott.com

Dedication:

*To all who believe that the human being is what
he was raised on, and probably he is not guilty of what he is,
he doesn't deserve to be killed on identity.*

.

Table of Contents:

Chapter Nine 181

Chapter Ten 219

Translator's introduction

The presence of gypsies in the Iraqi society has always been controversial because they are ethnically, culturally, and behaviourally different from the mainstream Iraqi society. They have faced a lot of rejection, discrimination, persecution, and hatred. Due to my knowledge of the author, who is a fellow citizen of my town, and his outstanding academic skills, I have not found a more comprehensive and better book dealing with the issue of gypsies and the way they adapt to Iraqi society like this book. The author has dealt with the issue of gypsies in Iraq, specifically with the study samples of Al Fawwar and Kamaliya, using sober fieldwork research methods.

When translating a book like this, you need to be careful about the names, concepts and terms contained in it. The author traced the names and origins of the gypsies and their spread in Iraq and with modern scientific methods, he addressed the way they adapt and deal with the host society. I had to follow these concepts and be accurate in transferring the vocabulary and the terms by going through the sources used by the author to give the accurate meaning of these terms and the concepts. The author has been a great help to me in this regard, as he showed the utmost cooperation throughout the work and during our correspondence and e-mails.

My town is not far from the Fawwar gypsy area. During the 1990s, gypsy female dancers were hired to conduct parties for the occasion of Saddam's birthday (the former Iraqi president) and the Baath Party establishment anniversary. I saw the dancers on a moving trailer among the crowds before going inside the Baath's HQ in the town to perform privately for the Baath's Party members. It was a way to adapt and practice the only profession they knew. I heard stories from people who visited the gypsy area revealing stories about their sexual experiences there. They claimed that they paid lots of money to get young gypsy girls for one night. A taxi driver told me about his experience with a gypsy woman who hired him. He said that she tried hard to seduce and tempt him and offered sex as a fee for the ride. But, as he said, he was aware of those wicked behaviours. He claimed that gypsy women often deceive taxi drivers offering sex instead of money as fees for the ride, but this kind of transaction often ended with ripping the drivers off and stealing all their money. After 2003 and the fall of Saddam's regime, the Fawwar gypsy area was raided by armed militias and gypsy families were displaced from the area. They went to Diwaniyah and lived there anonymously. Gypsy women, especially old ones, were seen begging in the streets.

The author was able to develop a unique theory about the origin of the gypsy group in Iraq and where they came from, it was a real challenge. However, he noted the eccentricity and isolation of this group, especially in the Fawwar area, and the number of social problems that erupted when they had contact and neighbourhood with the host community, as is the case in the Kamaliya area. I realized then that they did not belong to this society, rather they attempted to adapt over the years. It was a goal for him to write and a goal for me to translate.

The book is an important source that touches on the gypsies and deals with their origins, history, and integration. I had the honour to transfer it into English, especially since the gypsies are spread in many parts of the world to benefit researchers, writers and readers who do not speak Arabic.

Hassan Hadi

Foreword

By
Sarah Edgcumbe

Dr Hamied al Hashimi's sociological publications on issues such as minority identities and integration have been pored over by university students all over Iraq. Crucially, Dr al Hashimi's scholarship transcends established discourse concerning recognised minorities, to include socially ostracised, poorly understood, marginalised groups such as Iraqi Gypsies. As such, it is wonderful that with this English language translation, diligently and carefully produced by Mr Hassan Hadi, Dr al Hashimi's work on Iraqi Gypsies has now been made accessible to those who are not fortunate enough to understand Arabic. Beyond this English language publication representing increased accessibility of Iraqi sociological scholarship, it also constitutes a valuable contribution to the field of Romani Studies of Middle Eastern origin, as well as Romani Studies more broadly.

Romani studies is a stubbornly Eurocentric discipline, and as a result, very little published scholarship exists which focuses on Dom (Middle Eastern Roma) and Gypsies in the Middle East - particularly in Iraq. This book, originally published in Arabic in 2012, is the first comprehensive work of its kind to provide valuable insight into kinship networks, marriage dynamics, and economic practices among Iraqi Gypsies. Additionally, this book is notable because it represents an important milestone in Romani Studies literature, reflecting at once the geo-political environment, context, and time in which it was written. As such, it sheds light on a key stage in the trajectory and development of the field of Romani Studies. Though this book focuses on Iraqi Gypsies as the subject, it simultaneously enables the reader to glimpse the social and power dynamics in which both non-Gypsy researcher, and Gypsy subject are embedded. A vantage point from which to begin to understand the lived experience of Gypsies in Iraq, this book provides a foundation upon which to caution against homogenisation of Iraqi Gypsies and to promote ongoing ethnology-oriented research with one of Iraq's most maligned, and vulnerable minorities.

The position Dr al Hashimi adopts throughout this book sets him apart from the majority of his non-Gypsy Iraqi peers. Iraqi Gypsies have endured discrimination, marginalisation, and stigmatisation for decades, if not more. Iraqi state institutions and Iraqi society have consistently problematised Iraqi Gypsies (at least those who are not beloved singers and musicians) as irredeemably troublesome, culturally indecent, morally polluting non-citizens, who refuse to assimilate. As such, at various stages throughout Iraq's history, Iraqi Gypsies have been subjected to exclusion, exploitation, persecution, and discrimination. It is here that Dr al Hashimi diverges from many of his peers in recognising that far from being outsiders, or an exoticized, objectified 'Other', Gypsies are a deeply rooted component of the Iraqi social fabric, having been present in the country for centuries. Whereas Iraqi state institutions have historically deliberately excluded Gypsies from the benefits of full citizenship, consigning them to a marginal life characterised by precarity and poverty, Dr al Hashimi advocates for greater respect, understanding, and importantly, support, to overcome the entrenched socio-economic barriers to social cohesion which permeate Iraqi Gypsies' lives.

Just as this book contributes to an improved understanding of the lives and experiences of Iraqi Gypsies, so too does it present salient considerations concerning the ethics of conducting research and publishing work concerning marginalised minorities. Iraqi Gypsies, who have little recourse to any means through which to make their voices heard, are perpetually framed by socio-political discourse as dishonest and conniving. Such is the degree of derision reserved for Iraqi Gypsies, if they *were* to be provided with a platform from which to elevate their voices and concerns, they would likely be perceived by the Iraqi state and its public as untrustworthy and assumed to be distorting the truth in some way. Conducting research with Iraqi Gypsies is therefore socio-politically sensitive, but also laden with power imbalance. As non-Gypsy researchers, we analyse data and produce research as objectively as possible, but social science is inherently subjective and moments in time are innately transient. We cannot divorce ourselves from such subjectivity or transiency, as our entire world view is the cumulative sum of our life experiences, as is also the case for Gypsies. Researchers and scholars who are not Gypsy themselves, therefore bear a great deal of responsibility, and must be cautious of reinforcing or reproducing racist or prejudicial narratives through deployment of uncritical assumptions. Merely including Gypsies within our research as interviewees, or subjects of observation is insufficient if we do not ask the right questions, spend sufficient time with communities to contextualise their answers, or unveil the myriad ways in which power is deployed against them.

Violence is situated within power imbalance, as is evidenced by the complete exclusion of Iraqi Gypsies from political representation, their social ostracization, and the structural violence which saturates their everyday lives. Violence shapes their everyday interactions with non-Gypsies, influences (non)use of public space and services, permeates social networks, restricts opportunity, and limits Gypsy life through consignment to segregated, deplorable living conditions; poor access to health care; and obstruction of access to education and employment. The power differentials which incubate and (re)produce such forms of violence are evident in the relationship between Gypsies and the state, Gypsy and non-Gypsy public, and between (as well as within) Gypsy communities themselves. Similarly, the relationship between researcher and researched also presents a key locus for power analysis in terms of methodology used, questions employed, time committed to participants, participant selection, geographic area in which research is conducted, the process of analysis, and the acting of writing. Research participants have the power to withhold or manipulate information provided, but ultimately, the selection of information, the frame of analysis, and decisions concerning the degree of amplification or erasure of Gypsy voices is presided over by the researcher, who holds most of the power. Relatedly, we had the power to decide whether to interrogate, or ignore, the socio-political structures which both Gypsies and non-Gypsies inhabit, often with dramatically divergent experiences.

Popular discourse concerning Gypsies in Iraq conflates all Gypsies with sex work, or begging. Aside from this being a sweeping (false) generalisation, such discourse consistently fails to consider the structural violence, living conditions, and obstacles to other means of income generation which necessitate reliance on sex work and/ or begging in the first place. Similarly, reproduction of anti-Gypsy stereotypes which posit that Gypsies have no interest in education, fail to interrogate the barriers which prevent Gypsy children from accessing schools. As a result, symptoms of anti-Gypsyism are used to justify the continuance of anti-Gypsy social policies, while the root causes remain overlooked. This constitutes a discreet, often unrecognised form of political violence.

Political violence has firmly embedded itself in narratives and discourse concerning Iraq. Vast bodies of literature focus on U.S-led coalition assaults upon Iraqi human rights, private mercenary armies and their misdeeds, and a seemingly revolving door of militias, insurgents, and terrorist groups. However, more subtle, but arguably no-less devastating forms of political violence have received very little attention. For example, structural violence entails the state-imposed infliction of hidden forms of avoidable harm. Such harm can be devastating, and in the case of Iraqi Gypsies, has caused a significant inter-generational impact, trapping extended families in a cycle of circular poverty. Meanwhile, popular labelling of Gypsies by non-Gypsies animates the consequences of such structural violence and disproportionate poverty. The limited economic opportunities available to Iraqi Gypsies, and the corresponding dire poverty they often experience, have become essentialised in the public psyche, resulting in the deployment of labels which convey dehumanisation, homogenisation, and exclusion. In this way, labels tell a story of anti-Gypsyism which is mutually reinforced by society and state.

Throughout this book, Dr Al Hashimi stresses that Iraqi Gypsies are not a homogenous group. As such, he demonstrates a commitment to his interlocutors beyond that which would be expected of him by the Iraqi academy, or Iraqi society more generally. His contextually progressive scholarship advocates for Gypsies to be perceived as both human and citizen, two framings rarely applied in Iraq. This book therefore represents a divergence from long-standing socio-political norms which Other Iraqi Gypsies on the basis of their identity, and which ethnicise their poverty as a cultural or biological defect, or compulsion. By highlighting the severe and multifaceted nature of the discrimination Iraqi Gypsies face, Dr al Hashimi illuminates the barriers Gypsies face to poverty alleviation and integration: two things consistently demanded of them by a state which dehumanises and securitises them. The labels and discourse commonly applied to Gypsies in Iraq are indicative of a social dismissiveness towards anti-Gypsyism which is underpinned by contempt, and which reinforces the border between the Iraqi nation on the one hand, and Gypsies on the other.

The identity boundaries constructed by non-Gypsies in Iraq to differentiate, and distance themselves from Gypsies, are worthy of further research. These boundaries bolster socio-political dynamics which manufacture consent for structural violence against Iraqi Gypsies, enforcing their social positionality at the very bottom of the hierarchy of citizenship. It is therefore anti-Gypsyism which prevents Gypsies from being able to perform the roles demanded of them if they are to be accepted – or even tolerated within Iraqi society, rather than Gypsies themselves.

While this book provides much needed insight into the lives of Iraqi Gypsies, the motivations and dynamics which drive the (re)production of anti-Gypsy narratives in Iraq deserve equal attention. As Iraq enters it's 'post-conflict', post-ISIS peacebuilding phase, this book provides a platform from which to begin grappling with complexities such as how to address deeply embedded anti-Gypsyism in such a way as to promote equality in access to education, employment, and ultimately social cohesion. It also poses uncomfortable questions for those of us who, as non-Gypsy researchers speak for, or with, Gypsies, and who, as everyday people, may internalise anti-Gypsysim more than we should. This book gives us pause to reflect upon the everyday language we use, the political choices we make, and the media we consume.

It is my hope that this book will encourage researchers, journalists, scholars, and activists, to conduct research alongside Iraqi Gypsies, but equally that it will contribute towards a body of evidence which advocates for equality of service provision and the erosion of structural violence, ultimately enabling Iraqi Gypsies to speak for themselves – and be heard.

Sarah Edgcumbe

PhD Candidate, School of International Relations, University of St Andrews

December 2024.

Abstract:

In 2003, after the fall of the previous regime of Saddam Hussein in Iraq, the gypsies' houses were attacked by religious militias in many sites, and they cut off the electricity and destroyed the only school there. This situation threw light on the kind of relations between gypsies and their neighbours. The empirical socio-anthropological study investigates Gypsies as an international phenomenon and as a sub-culture in Iraqi society. It focuses on their social adaptation in Iraq.

The work is based on George Homans's theory of social exchange, which was enriched by Peter Blau, Thebot, and Kelly as a theoretical framework.

The essence of this theory is the process of balance between costs and profits that results from social interaction.

This study's approach is a case study that deals with units (individuals or groups). Here, the household is the study unit, as we depend on this approach (case study). The comparative, historical, and statistical methods are used.

This research concentrates on the Gypsies in two regions:

Kamaliya in Baghdad and Fawwar in Qadisiya province as patterns for other Gypsies groups all over the country.

These groups are:
1- Gypsies' village of Hammam El Alil (Mosul).
2- Gypsies' village of Taza (Kerkuk).
3- Gypsies' village of Kenan (Diala).
4- Gypsies' village of Abu Ghraib (Baghdad).
5- Gypsies' village of Shomali (Babil).
6- Gypsies' village of Shatra (Nasiriya).
7- Gypsies' village of Fajir (Nasiriya).
8- Gypsies' village of Zubair (Basra).

However, the two regions mentioned above (Kamaliya & Fawwar) have standard features and suitable patterns in all other areas. Besides, they represent the places of activities and polarisation for a long time.

Methodological techniques used are:

1- Interviews 2- Observation 3- Tellers 4- data and documents.

The study has two sides: theoretical and practical (fieldwork).

The theoretical part has two chapters; the first is on the research frames and background, while the second is an introduction to the Gypsies study and it has a considerable hypothesis that the word (Kawliya) which means (Gypsies) in Iraq, dates back to the king (Kawil) in India.

The fieldwork part has six chapters: the first deals with the relationship system, from studying the family, relationships, and the suitable status of the woman as a result of her economic role.

The family size in Kamaliya was (10.2) souls against (9) souls in Fawwar.

The chapter also discusses the weakness of relations among relatives.

Chapter two focuses on the religious system and that all the Gypsies are Muslims and this is a kind of social adaptation or integration.

Chapter three deals with economic activities, including singing, music, dance, sex trade (sex work) and bar business. The chapter also shows the importance of women in these activities.

Chapter four studies social control according to its main elements: law, religion and mores. It indicates that the most influential kind of control is the law (police).

Chapter five deals with cultural communication, and it shows that cultural connection is more active in Kamaliya than in Fawwar, and this in turn refers to the contact with the society of Baghdad.

Chapter six focuses on social adaptation, which is divided into two types: adaptation in form (appearance), like fashions, religion, language and habits of eating and drinking. This type of adaptation is an identical adaptation (from one side). Adaptation, in essence, is closely related to the relation of affinity (interracial marriage), friendship, and neighbourhood. The latter needs two sides (Gypsies & no Gypsies).

The last chapter throws light on the current situation of gypsies in Iraq after the fall of Saddam Hussein's regime and the domination of religious militias and parties.

Finally, the research consists of suggestions and recommendations, among them:

Gathering Gypsies in certain places with considerable services, especially entertainment services and directing the Gypsies to certain jobs like agriculture so they could practice easily and need not certain skills.

The study suggests also supplying Gypsies communication with healthy censorship and security means.

Introduction

Whenever Gypsies are mentioned—by any of their various local names and in any country around the world—the term often provokes curiosity due to the strangeness, mystery, and attraction associated with their way of life. Their existence is surrounded by countless stories, theories, and prejudices, which collectively contribute to a stereotypical image that precedes them wherever they go or are spoken of.

Gypsies have long inspired, and continue to inspire, poets, singers, and lovers of freedom and spontaneity. Their lives—characterized by constant movement, joyfulness, and various artistic expressions such as singing and dancing—are often linked to ideals of freedom and nonconformity. Numerous theories exist concerning their origins, migration routes, and whether they descend from a single race or multiple ethnic groups.

As a subject, Gypsies offer rich material for social and anthropological research due to their unique cultural traits, which shape most aspects of their lifestyle. Their social nature is remarkably adaptable, absorbing many features of the societies they enter, including language, religion, and customs. At the same time, they preserve distinct characteristics—especially in livelihood, residence, and belief systems—that set them apart.

Gypsies live in many parts of the world: they roam across Europe, the Americas, African deserts, and Asian farmlands. They often consider themselves a mystery—one that outsiders cannot easily penetrate.

This study provides a general overview of Gypsies, focusing on their definitions, origins, and global nomenclature. It pays particular attention to the Gypsies of Iraq, known locally as **Kawliya**, by investigating the origin of this term. The author proposes a new theory about the name's origin, diverging from existing, commonly accepted theories. The study also examines the geographical distribution of the Kawliya in Iraq.

The Kawliya have faced aggression and displacement by armed religious militias and terrorist groups that emerged after the fall of the regime following the 2003 war and occupation of Iraq. These attacks were justified by accusations of the Kawliya's moral deviance and behaviours deemed incompatible with Iraq's conservative culture. As a result, their already precarious lives became even more difficult, plunging them into conditions more dire than those they had previously endured—as will be demonstrated in this study.

The central focus of this fieldwork is the **social adaptation** of the Kawliya. The study of social adaptation involves an analysis of the entire social structure of the community under investigation. Therefore, this research explores the key systems that are directly related to social adaptation, including kinship, economic and religious structures, as well as social discipline. It also examines communication and social interaction and evaluates adaptation as an independent variable by analysing the extent to which it manifests across different aspects of Kawliya life.

It is important to distinguish between **social adaptation** and **social integration**. Social integration implies the abandonment of many traditions, practices, and values of a minority group in favour of conforming to the dominant culture. In exchange, individuals from the minority may gain greater opportunities and access within the larger society. In contrast, **social adaptation** often involves surface-level or strategic changes made by individuals or groups to reduce social friction and avoid negative reactions to their distinct cultural practices, without fully assimilating.

The first chapter raises theoretical questions concerning the classification of Gypsies as an ethnic minority and explores the various names attributed to them globally. The second chapter examines several hypotheses about their racial origins and discusses the shared characteristics of Gypsy groups across different regions, including a section on the Gypsies and the Holocaust.

The third chapter introduces the topic of Gypsies by exploring their commonly used names, racial hypotheses, and estimated global population. It also investigates the presence of the **Kawliya** in Iraq, including their arrival in the country and current locations.

The field research comprises seven chapters:
- **Chapter Four** analyses the kinship system in three parts: household structure (covering family size, gender distribution, education, etc.), kinship ties and the status of relatives, and finally, marriage practices and associated rituals.
- **Chapter Five** explores the religious system, examining the role of religion in Kawliya life, their level of religious observance, and how their occupations may conflict with religious norms.

- **Chapter Six** discusses the economic system, with emphasis on primary occupations such as entertainment (singing, music, and dance), sex work (including the role of pimps), and other commercial activities like shop ownership or management.
- **Chapter Seven** deals with social discipline and the internal forces that regulate individual behaviour within the community.
- **Chapter Eight** focuses on urban communication and social interaction, including communication styles, their effects, and the resulting forms of social engagement—especially in terms of how this influence adaptation.
- **Chapter Nine** centres on social adaptation itself, presenting examples of adaptation achieved by the Kawliya and comparing adaptation levels between the two study areas.
- **Chapter Ten** addresses issues related to the Kawliya's housing and neighbourhood conditions following the political transformations in Iraq after 2003. It concludes with suggestions and recommendations for addressing their current situation and exploring potential long-term solutions.

The Gypsies, or Kawliya, represent a **distinct subculture** that stands in contrast to Iraq's dominant cultural norms and values. They remain a source of fascination—and, for many, a mystery—that continues to attract both the public and academic researchers.

Chapter One

Who are the gypsies or Kawliya?

Are the gypsies an ethnic group?

The names of the gypsies in the world.

Hypotheses in gypsies' Origin

Common characteristics of the gypsies in the world

Are Gypsies an ethnic group?

Morris defines the ethnic group as a distinct category of people living in a bigger community; this category has a distinct culture and feels independent. It is coherent either by their ancestry, culture, or nationality. On his part, Schermerhorn defines the ethnic group as a group of people who live in a bigger community sharing one ancestor (one ancestry), one history and the same memories based on one or more symbolic elements which make them feel their peoplehood. Among these elements are blood relationships, neighbourhood, physical contact, language, different accents, tribalism and tribal or religious belonging or any structure of these elements[1].

Barth believes that the ethnic group is a group of people that could be identified through the following characteristics:
1. Having a special ancestral situation distinguishes them from other groups.
2. Sharing elements, features, and civilized patterns.
3. Having its own special structure of ways of communication and internal interaction among its members and between the entire group and other individuals.
4. The individuals of the group are distinct, due to having independent personalities through their group membership and belonging. At the same time, they are also members of some of the other organisations within the society. [2]

---

[1] Ismail, Farooq, Social Relationships Among Ethnic groups, 3rd edition, Qatari Ben Al Fuja'a publishing house, Qatar 1986, 42.
[2] Al Ani, Muzahim, Communication and its role in the social change, doctoral thesis in Greek (not published) introduced to <u>Pandious</u> Greek University, 1992.

From all that, we conclude that an ethnic group is a group or a minority which has civilised features, either racial, lingual, religious, sectarian or even professional or most of these features. This group lives in a wider community, and these features make them distinct from that community to form a subculture.

Depending upon that and according to the racial and cultural features of the gypsies all over the world and particularly in Iraq; we can reach a conclusion here which is that they are a subculture and an ethnic group [3] in the Iraqi community.

Gypsies' names in the world:

The gypsies have multiple names which are different from one country to the other and from one region to the other all over the world. They acquire these names either from the gypsies themselves or from other peoples whom they pass by or live among. These names vary according to their sources, either the source is the gypsies themselves claiming to be honourable and deep-rooted or to be named by others giving a false assumed impression about them based on either their

---

[3] Morris defines the ethnic group as a distinct category of people living in a bigger community, this category has a distinct culture and feels independent, and it is coherent either by their ancestry, culture, or nationality. On his part, Schermerhorn defines the ethnic group as a group of people who live in a bigger community sharing one ancestor (one ancestry), one history and the same memories based on one or more symbolic elements that make them feel with their peoplehood. Among these elements are blood relationships, neighbourhood, physical contact, language, different accents, tribalism and tribal or religious belonging or any structure of these elements. (Ismail, Farooq, ibid, 42)

activities by which they are known, the place from which they came, their physical characteristics or on their culture.

Here we look over the major and common names in the world and discuss some of them and their sources.

Gypsies: Ghajar:

The word (gypsy) is originally an Indian word as there is an Indian language called Gujarati [4] which was mentioned by Gibson, a professor of linguistics, in research about learning languages and the difficulty of the Indian languages. [5]

Most researchers, who work on gypsies or what is called (Gypsology), agree that they belong to an Indian race, and they migrated in waves towards the west and the north passing through the middle east. They are the only people that India introduced to Europe during the last three thousand years, compared to the people that came from Europe to India. Lots of gypsies are still living in India as they are in almost every country in the world. [6]

Howard Greenfield believes that gypsies are real Bedouins roaming from one place to the other with no need for settling down and they do not want to join a permanent settled community. These people do

---

4   Probably goes back to Gujarat territory in India.

5   Sheikh Ali, Khalil, A Stop on Kawliya Ways, Al-Balad newspaper of Baghdad, issue (353), July 9th, 1965.

6   Arif, Majeed Hameed, Cultures and Peoples, Al-Kutub Publishing House, Baghdad, 1993, p.199.

not have any traditions, and there are lots of ideas which are inspired by supernatural powers. [7]

We do not agree with Howard Greenfield's point of view concerning the gypsies being real Bedouins. I believe that they are semi-Bedouins since the gypsies in Iraq, as instance, stopped roaming and settled down in settlements in different parts of Iraq as we will see that later. In addition, their living features are different from those of the real Bedouins.

Gypsies are coloured Caucasian people, who originally came from India and reached Europe in the fourteenth and fifteenth centuries. Now, they can mainly be found in Turkey, Russia, England, and the United States of America. [8]

Gypsy individuals (concerning Egypt) are people who refer to the life of roaming, wandering and homeless people whose women are dishonest. They are bronze-coloured Bedouin people with black hair. They are originally Indian, and now they are globally known. Their language is Romani. [9]

Among viewpoints about the origin and name of gypsies, is what the gypsologist Mr. Lutfi Al Khuri mentioned:

---

7   Greenfield, Howard. Gypsies, Crown Publishers. Inc. New York, 1977, P.1.
8   Webster's Third New International Dictionary, vol. 1, A.G. P. 61.
9   New Webster Dictionary, P.20.

The word (Ghajar) is a Turkish utterance taken from "Gocher", which means "nomadic" because up till now, some people call them by this name in the north of Mosul (Iraq), and others call them (Qarach). [10]

According to another point of view, (Ghajar) is derived from (Qajari), referring to a Turkish-origin tribe, from which the extinct royal family in Iran descended, and so, the (Qajari) is not the (Kawli), and it is not right to call the (Kawli) a (Qajari) [11] The gypsies reached Europe during the Middle Ages and probably they were originally Indian. The Nazis oppressed this European group, even though, by their racial theories, this group had a greater claim than any other European race to be considered Aryan. [12]

The gypsies are the Bedouins who migrated to Europe coming from the east, traditionally from India, in the fourteenth century and they claim that they belong to several different peoples. [13]

Most of these opinions agree that the race of the gypsies is Indian, but they disagree about the name. For us, the word "gypsy" is a local name which is used in the official records and media, this name is given to people who make dancing, singing and sex work as their jobs. They settled down in settlements near bigger cities, whereas they had been roaming until the early seventies. They were granted Iraqi citizenship in the early eighties; the local people called them "Kawliya".

---

10   *Jean-Paul* Clebert, Gypsies: A historical and Folklore study, Translated by Lutfi Al-Khuri, Cultural Affairs House, Baghdad, 1976, P.361
11   Ibid, P.360
12   Manchip, White, Anthropology English Universities press, London, 1954. P.64
13   The Encyclpedia Americana, International Education, vol. 13, New York, 1976. P. 646.

Kawliya

It's a local name for gypsies in Iraq, and sometimes it is pronounced like "Kewliya" while the single of it is " Kawli".

We presented several hypotheses about the origin and source of this name as well as its explanation. Dr Mustafa Jawad, an Iraqi researcher, believes that "Kawliya" refers to Kabul, the capital of Afghanistan, i.e., it has a Kabuli origin. Their name goes back to India, but they got this name when they passed Sind going to Iran, Kabul lies on the western gateway of the Khyber Pass linking Sind and Afghanistan. [14]

This opinion is the most common to explain this name, and it is somewhat reasonable, but we believe that there were lots of immigration waves. These waves passed through this way and there is no doubt that they all passed through Kabul since Khyber is the main gateway through. Some of them might camp to get some rest for days and then they continued their immigration journeys. The question is: why didn't they catch names like Kabuli or Kawli? This is why there are doubts and questions about this assumption, because we know that the Kawliya is just one of gypsy tribes or groups, and there are similar and close gypsy groups but with different names.

Father Anstas Mary Al Karmali [15] believes that the word "Kol" (Kawli) belongs to an evil unbeliever sect which settled in the Multan

---

[14]   Jawad, Mustafa, The gypsies in Arabic resources, Arab Kuwaiti Magazine, vol. 126, May 1969, P. 40.

[15]   An Iraqi researcher, born in Baghdad in August 1866, his father Is originally from Karmil Mount in Lebanon, he worked on Arabic language and Arabic literature, and he issued "Lisan Al-Arab" and "Lugat Al-Arab" magazines (1911-1932).

district in Pakistan. He thinks that "Kol" or "Kawliya" is derived from "Takawwul", which means gathering, or it refers to Kol, which is a village in Persia. [16]

Shakir Al Dhabit, referring to Lutfi Al-Khuri, believes that it means "Kawool" and its Turkish meaning is "ruined" and "Kawli" in Turkish means "the one who left his house and became a roamer". [17]

"Kawli", as mentioned in the Persian dictionary "Farhang Anandraj", is a synonym for "Lori", which is another name for gypsies, used to call a group of Indians while the "a" was omitted in the Persian language to become "Kwli".[18]

Khalil Al Sheikh Ali believes, in an article in Al Balad Baghdadi newspaper vol. 353 in 1965, that the word "Kalia", which is not a Spanish word and used to call them in Spain, came from Indian languages, from the original Kawliya (gypsy) accents and it came to Spain from India. [19]

We exclude the latter viewpoint as we weaken those before it because the origin of Kawliya is the East although there is a convergence of naming between Kawliya of Iraq and those of Spain. Probably "Kalia" is the corrupted form of Kawliya, while the latter is precedent in time

---

16 Hassan, Ali, Baghdadi Al-Turath Al-Shaabi magazine, vol.2, in 1-18 September 1968.
17 Caliber, OP Cit., P 3.
18 Al-Hadithi, Taha Hamadi, Gypsy and Qarach in Iraq, printed by Mosul University, 1979, P16.
19 Durant, Will, The Story of Civilization: Our Heritage, part 3, Vul. 1, Simon & Schuster, New York, 1942, Pp. 490-491.

and place, and that is an agreement about the source, which is the east, India, and about the name, which is "Kawliya".

So, what does "Kawliya" mean?

Our new hypothesis about the name "Kawliya":

After researching in the origin of the name and looking over what was written about the History of India and Indian tribes, we concluded that this name is applied to Indian tribes who's some women do sex work and dancing as a religious free service for religious men and a paid service for enjoyment seekers, some of that were in **King Chola Temple**.

They affiliated with King Chola, especially after they immigrated to honour and glorify themselves. There is a clear text by which we can infer Kawliya's name and race. This text is what was written by the researcher Will Durant in his book "The Story of Civilization". Their immigration to the Middle East, especially to Iraq, came after their fellows of other previous tribes, which came, as the poet Firdausi said, on the request of the Persian Shah.

This text, which was written by Will Durant in his great book "The Story of Civilization" in the section on India and its neighbours, in the chapter "Community organisation, marriage, sex work, and others", Durant said:[20]

---

[20] Ibid, Pp. 490-491.

"Sex work was, for the most part, confined to the temples. In the south, the needs of the esurient male were met by the providential institution of devadasis, literally "servants of the gods," sex workers. Each Tamil temple had a troop of "sacred women," engaged at first to dance and sing before the idols, and perhaps to entertain the Brahmans. Some of them seem to have lived lives of almost conventional seclusion; others were allowed to extend their services to all who could pay, on condition that a part of their earnings should be contributed to the clergy. Many of these temple courtesans, or nautch girls, provided dancing and singing in public functions and private gatherings, in the style of the geishas of Japan; some of them learned to read, and, like the hetaerae of Greece, furnished cultured conversation in homes where the married women were neither encouraged to read nor allowed to mingle with guests. In 1004 A.D., as a sacred inscription informs us, the temple of the Chola King Rajaraja at Tanjore had four hundred devadasis. acquired the sanctity of time, and no one seems to have considered it immoral; respectable women now and then dedicated a daughter to the profession of temple sex worker in much the same spirit in which a son might be dedicated to the priesthood".

There is no doubt that this text is considered as evidence denoting and emphasizing on the name of the gypsies as well as on their race.

Qarach:

Benjamin believes that "Qarach" is derived from the Turkish word "Qara", which means "black". In addition, the French name for gypsies (Tsigane) also refers to the distinct black colour and it refers to the connection between the gypsies and the Qarach too. Father

(Anastas Al Karmali) believes that their name is used to call a group of Nawar people who live in the suburbs of Mosul and some parts of Baghdad. These people are characterized by greed and theft, and they claim to belong to Al Qurayshiyeen, whereas they probably came from Qarach town, which lies between Hamadan and Esfahan. Father Karmali believes that they almost belong to a Persian or Turkish race. " Qarachi", according to a Turkish dictionary, is a synonym for Ghajari, which means "immoral". These people are idol worshippers who grew up in India, and then part of them spread to Iran, Iraq, and Egypt, while another part of them were distributed in France and Spain (French land and Andalusia), living a Bedouin life. This dictionary also mentioned that "Qarchi" is derived from "Qarachi", which means a thief or a bandit. [21]

Taha Hamadi Al Hadithi emphasizes the latter opinion, saying that "Qarachi" is a name for a jaundiced kind of behaviour and not for black colour or a name of a city as most Iraqis use this name to call a ribald person. [22]

We believe that Al Hadithi's opinion might not be correct due to its weakness. Calling ribald people by Qarachi (as a disparaging adjective) comes (as an adjective) because of their behaviour (Qarachi). If their name were different, the disparaging adjective would have been the same, taking the other name too. But if their adjective was good, it wouldn't have been used to vilify others. As proof for this, in the south of Iraq, "Kawli" is used for calling a bad person the same way

---

21   Al-Hadthi, Op Cit., P.P. 20-21.
22   Ibid, P. 21.

as "Qarachi" is used, but Qarachi is almost unknown in the middle and south of Iraq.

" Qarachi" might be "Karaki" or "Karaghi' which was the earliest name used by the Persians to call the gypsies, in addition, gypsies in Azerbaijan were called Karaki which is a Turkish word meaning "a beggar". [23]

Anyway, Qarach in Iraq had some cultural similarities with the gypsies of Iraq for a short time before being settled down and moving from their traditional jobs into what they are now.

It is not right to call them gypsies as we do to the gypsies of Iraq beside that they wouldn't accept that. They adapt and integrate fast within the community; in addition, their presence is not necessarily as distinct as that of the gypsies, so we will restrict our study to the gypsies only.

Taha Al Hadithi believes that Qarach is a mixture of multiple human groups, like Kurds, Turks, Arabs, and other peoples that came to Iraq from Iran and Turkey during unknown periods, which could not be identified. [24]

Qarach is a gypsy group living in the northern parts of Iraq and they are also called (Persian Kawliya) to be distinguished from Kawliya. Qarachi families camping in Telafar claim to belong to the Bani Murra Arab tribe. [25]

---

23 Ibid, P. 75.
24 Al-hadithi, Op Cit, P21.
25 Ibid, P.P. 21-22.

Al Nawar:

It's a word used to describe gypsy groups in Arab countries like Lebanon, Palestine, Syria, and Jordan. Nabeel Subhi Hanna, who is specialized in gypsology, believes that "Nawar" means a thief, or a hustler and he believes that it does not stand as a synonym for "Gypsies" in English. This word also means a clown or a comic. [26]

But we believe that it is one of their many local names, which is a result of either their features or behaviour or where they came from or because of a specific occasion.

There is a possibility that "Nawar" is derived from "Noori", but Quatremère believes that it is derived from the Arabic noun "Nar" or the Arabic verb "Nawer" as they always carry an ember, niche or lantern or because their work with heat. There is another possibility that "Nawar" can be found in the Sanskrit dialect of the northern west part of India which is considered as the homeland of gypsy groups. [27]

Jean-Paul Clébert believes that "Lawari" became "Noori" which is used to call a group of Bedouins living in Syria, Egypt and Palestine, or it belongs to the Arabic word "Noor" and used to name the gypsies living in Arab countries. [28]

---

26 Hanna, Nabeel Subhi, Gypsy Groups with a Special Reference to the Gypsies in Egypt and Arab Countries, 1st edition, Al-Maarif publishing house, Egypt, 1980, P 272.
27 Ibid, P. 292
28 Clebert, Op Cit, P.37.

Lawar:

It is one of gypsies' names and it is the name of the first and the oldest gypsy tribe which came from Iran in the fifth century AD. [29] It is also the original name of the Indian tribe, and they are also called "Luli". Al Firdausi, the poet, said in Al Shahnama that they were the tribe, which was sent by Sankar, the king of India, to the Persian king Bahram Gur. According to his request, they were ten thousand in number. [30]

Khalil Al Sheikh Ali believes that "Luri" is the origin of "Nawar" which is common in Jordan and Syria [31] while Al Hadithi thinks that Lore tribe is the ancestor of the gypsies, and it was roaming beside working in music and singing business. [32]

There is no doubt that Lore is less influential and prominent in the communities in which they live as it is with the gypsies in Iraq.

Gengene:

Gemgene or Gengecan is the gypsies' name in Turkey, they do dance and singing. This word is used by common people in Mosul (Iraq), and it means a light or jaunty person, and it refers to the zither (Genk) player. Malcolm believes that "Gengene", like "Kauole", refers to musical business and carelessness ", immoral corruption". [33]

---

29   Ibid, p. 37.
30   Al Hadithi, P16.
31   Sheikh Ali, P3.
32   Al-Hadithi, P19.
33   Ibid, P182.

Zutt:

Al Sihah Arabic dictionary stated that Zutt is a generation of people, a single person of them is called Zutti.[34] Zutt is the old name of the gypsies in Iraq and the neighbouring areas.

In a lecture in the royal academy in Amsterdam (December 11th, 1975), De Foy, the orientalist, stated that the gypsies, known by (Tsigane) in France and Zutt in Arab countries, came from the west of India and most of them belong to the Jit tribe that lived near West Multan. Mustafa Jawad agrees with De Foy about "Zutt" name being the oldest name for the gypsies or "Kawliya" in Iraq. They were known for the first time in Iraq during the reign of Al Hajjaj Bin Yussif Al Thaqafi, the Umayyad governor in the early seventh century AD. When they occupied Sindh, Arab fighters brought lots of Zutts to Iraq and Al Hajaj resettled them with their animals, especially buffalos in the south of Kaskar.

In Al Mamoon's era, they started robbing goods cargos in the Tigris between Basra and Baghdad, but when Al Mustaasem Billah came to reign in 833 AD, he assigned Ujaif Bin Unbissa to fight them, and the latter defeated them and took them to Baghdad and then moved some of them to Khanaqeen and some others to Aen Zirba and Al Thughoor. In one of their raids on Ain Zirba in 855 AD, the Romans invaded the Zutt and moved them with their women, children and animals, especially buffaloes, to Byzantium and they were the first gypsy group which were moved to Europe across the Bosporus. [35]

---

[34] Al-Razi, Abu Bakr, Mukhtar Al Sihah dictionary, Vol.1, Dar Al-Risala, Kuwait, 1986, p. 271.

[35] Al-Hadithi, PP 18-19.

Al Hadithi thinks that there are no convincing pieces of evidence proving that the Zutt were the ancestors of the gypsies in Iraq. The name was not restricted to a specific first emigrated group coming from Sindh to Iraq, but it was used to name all Sindh-coming people. The Zutts were a settled group known for breeding buffalo in Sindh. The Muslims brought these animals to the marshes area in the south of Iraq. Other resources state that " Lore" is the origin of the gypsiess. [36]

We agree with Al Hadithi's opinion because the gypsies never knew a job other than their famous ones by which they were known like music and singing, metal works, horoscope reading and things related to that. Studies and research showed that they never knew stability, but since the buffalo breeding job required stability and had a unique environment, which could not be found anywhere else in other neighbouring areas, we believe in the exactitude of Al Hadithi's point of view mentioned earlier, especially when we read in Ahmed Bin Yahia Al Balatheri's book: Fateh Al Futooh that the Zutt and the ancient Al Sayanija reached Levant (Syria) and Antioch during Muaawiyah reign. Al-Waleed Bin Abdul-Malik also moved some of the Zutt to Antioch. [37]

In Abul Fadhil Jamalu-Deen's book: Lisan Al Arab and under item Zuttat, he mentioned: "Zuttat, Zutt, a black human generation to whom Zutt leadership belongs … and they were an Indian generation."[38]

---

[36]   Ibid, P 19.
[37]   Clebert, P 351.
[38]   Ibid, P. 353.

Al Qufs:

It is and old name for the gypsies, it is mentioned in Abul Fadhil Bin Mandhoor's Lisan Al Arab dictionary that they were a group of people living in one of Karman mountains. In Al Tahtheeb; Qufs is a generation living in Karman suburbs, they have experienced war. [39] In the Persian translation margin of the Al Muheet dictionary, Qufs was mentioned to be a communion translated into Arabic to be Kinj or Kunj and sometimes Kofjan. [40]

On the other hand, Dr. Mustafa Jawad thinks that "Qufs" refers to the English word "gypsy" which means that "gypsy" is originally an Arabic word. [41]

Halab

It is one of the local names for gypsies in Egypt, they spread in different parts of Egypt. Some assume that their name is connected to Aleppo in Syria. It is said that they called themselves "Mahleebish", and probably they derived the latter name from "Halab" (Aleppo). Theopold stated that the tribes of this group, like "Kostani", disbanded in Abyssinia under other names.

---

[39] Ibid, P. 352
[40] Ibid, P. 358
[41] Ibid, P. 358

Al Qurbat or Ghurbat

This name is for gypsies in Afghanistan, Greece, Syria, and Lebanon. Scientists disagree about the origin of this name, some of them say that it goes back to an Arabic origin (Ghurba) while others consider it a Persian name (Ghurab) which means to be absent from home or non-attendance. [42]

Kalderash:

They are the only group of people to be thought a pure gypsy group. They are, as they say, blacksmiths before anything else, they work in tin and copper. Kalderash, as a word, means "boiler or frying pan" in Romney and Spanish languages. They recently came from Balkan countries and later from the middle of Europe and then they broke up into five groups: [43]

1. Lufari: called (Mariners) in France since they came from the sea.
2. Yowiha: came from Transylvania.
3. Regardless of whether it's 'Lorry' or 'Lolly,' the name still refers to the Indian tribe mentioned by Firdausi".
4. Shiyoradi: they separated from Kalderash gypsies.
5. The American Turkish: called so, because they migrated from Turkey to America before they returned and forth to Europe. [44]

---

42 Djuric, Op Cit, P68.
43 Hannah, Op Cit., P68
44 Ibid, P. 68

Kalderash is thought to be the chiefs of other gypsies and to have a high status that made them refuse to marry their women to other gypsies' men whereas they marry other gypsies' women. [45]

Khitanos:

This group can be found in Spain, the north of Africa, Portugal, and the south of France. They are different from Kalderash in physical appearance as well as accent and traditions. They are subdivided into Gitanos, Spanish, Kathmas and Andalusian. [46]

Manosh:

They are traditional Bohemian people, their name means (the originals) in the Sanskrit language. They are also called Sinti because they are Indian in origin and passed by the Sind coast. They are subdivided into several sub-groups:
1. Vale Cigana or Cini, the French travellers who work for theatres and companies.
2. G Gicans: they mixed with the European Yesh Edo, which is considered a part of gypsy ancestries, but they live with the same gypsy traditions. [47]

---

45   Ibid, P. 68
46   Ibid, P. 69
47   Ibid, P. 69-70

Tsigane:

It is one of the gypsies' names in some European countries; in Dutch, it is "Zigeuner" and "Zigeuner" in Polish whereas it is "Cigany" in German, Ciganie in Roman, Cigany in Greek and Zingaro in Italian while in Spanish Sikan is also used. Correspondently, Khalil Al Sheikh said: the gypsies in Spain were wrongly named "Tsigane", what I well remember is that "Tsigane" is a word, dancing in my mind with the Flamingo music during the dance and singing peak to stimulate the singer and dancer or to enflame gleesome. Linguists believe that this utterance is of an Indian root, close to Sanskrit, which does not refer to any kind of gypsies in modern Spain. [48]

Bohemian:

It is a mane used to call gypsies in Scandinavian countries and some other European countries. This name roots back to Bohemia where they first appeared in Europe. [49] Bohemia, as we all know, is a Hungarian territory, and maybe there is a direct connection between its name and these gypsies since huge number of gypsies live in Hungary.

Gypsy:

American Encyclopaedia claims that "Gypsies" was derived from "Egyptian" and was widely used in English tradition to identify a

---

[48] Sheikh Ali, op. cit., P 3
[49] Ibid, P 3

group of people having certain ethnographic characteristics among which are having light blond hair, constant travelling all over the world beside illiteracy and adopting the tribal system. Thomas Acton believes that "Gypsy" is an abbreviation for "Egyptian" taking into consideration that the first people who came to England in the fifteenth century declared that they came from Egypt.

Dr Mustafa Jawad disagreed with the above opinion stating that "Gypsy" is not related to "Egypt". He believes that it is just a fabrication meant to offend the Eastern peoples in general and the Egyptians in particular. He believes that this name is close to "Qufs" who were displaced from Karman, their original homeland, in 967 AD by Aḍud Al Dawla Al Buwaihi because they spread corruption in the area. So, they immigrated to Europe, and that made the English call them "Gypsy". [50]

But Howard Greenfield says, people in Europe saw Gypsies for the first time in the early Middle Ages of the fifteenth century through Germany. Clergies, rulers, and other people warmly welcomed them since they asked for sympathy and mercy. In 1422 AD, they first appeared in Bologna, Italy, under the command of the president who called himself the Duke Michel of Egypt with a hundred men, women, and children. They settled near a city gate. [51]

In Grolier Encyclopaedia, "Gypsy" was referred to as many or few Bedouins or groups of people of about one million or one million and a half in number spread in Europe, America, North Africa, West

---

[50]   Al-Hadithi, Op Cit., P 15.
[51]   Greenfield, Op Cit, P. 12-13.

Asia and only countries which speak English. Those people are called "Gypsy" which was derived from "Egyptian" due to the traditional construction with which they originally came from Egypt. [52]

The latest viewpoint emphasizes that "Gypsies", which are considered Egyptians, are restricted to countries that speak English or what is called the Anglo-Saxon or the British Commonwealth. The author of this encyclopaedia does not frankly declare that they were Egyptian, but they illustrated that they had certain entities which could be cultural or physical. If it was cultural, it means they were not Egyptian, they only conveyed the heritage, and they were only transmitters. But if it is physical, there is no doubt that he means they were Egyptian.

Zigeuners

It is the utterance used to identifies the gypsies in Holland where they form a minority. This name may be derived from "Tsigane" or any close gypsy name which was common in Germany, Bologna, Italy... etc.

---

[52] Grolier, Encyclopaedia, vol. 10, Distributed by the Grolier Incorp Orated, New York, 1961, P. 100.

Chapter Two

Hypotheses in gypsies' origin

Conclusion

The gypsies' common characteristics all over the world

Gypsies and Holocaust

Hypotheses in Gypsies' Origin:

Gypsies are among the most (displaced) people and are subject to trouble. Wherever they go, their real or exaggerated reputation precedes them. They are considered unwanted guests by lots of people due to the nature of their life besides their work and the distorted images that may corrupt their reputation.

Their negative reputation might be at the formal or informal levels or in the epistemological circles. As proof of this common negative viewpoint, we may refer to gypsies' definition in the Chic Language Dictionary, published in Prague in 1952, in this definition gypsies are described as wandering people who take lying and theft as a profession besides being jugglers and cheaters, despite their serious tries, in most of the times, to adapt to the societies they adjoin or live in.

Gypsies were subject to waves of oppression and extermination throughout their history, probably the latest one was the Nazi extermination campaigns against them as what happened to the Jews as we all know.

Gypsies believe that they are the masters of Earth and the free people as well as the symbol of love and romance. So, where do these people come from? And is there any proof of their race?

We read and heard about lots of hypotheses concerning gypsies' race and the areas they came from. These viewpoints differed in identifying gypsies' race. Researchers, who are interested in gypsology, and even gypsies themselves, do not agree on specific dates for the beginning of their immigration. There are several myths about their origin and belonging, but most opinions agree that India is their origin.

Some other opinions state that gypsies' origin goes back to Egypt and Iraq, while less common one's state that Palestine is their origin.

Perhaps the most important opinions and hypotheses about gypsies' homeland are:

Palestine:

This opinion relies on certain myths, among which were explained in the Old Testament, believing that they belonged to Cain's cursed strain. According to one of these myths, when Jesus Christ was crucified, four nails were needed, blacksmiths refused to make them due to the emergence of his major miracles, but the gypsies made them at last under the effect of money temptation. [53]

Jean-Paul Clebert sees weakness in this hypothesis saying that it is a mere illusion and up till this moment no proof sustains gypsies' existence in Palestine during the first century AD. He also believes that these people desire to have their roots. On his part, Philant believes that they have a Phoenician race, but this hypothesis remains weak due to its weak support and unscientific basis.

---

[53] Clebert, op. cit., P. 18-19.

Egypt:

"Gypsy", as a term, refers to gypsies and is common in use in the Anglo-Saxon system, it was derived from "Egypt" due to the common belief that they were Egyptians. This opinion is sustained by what is mentioned in Grolier Encyclopaedia although "gypsy", which derived from Egypt because of the traditional construction they came with originally from Egypt, is used to call gypsies only in speaking English countries (according to the encyclopaedia). [54]

Howard Greenfield believes that they appear for the first time in Bologna, Italy in 1422 under the leadership of the president who called himself the Duke of Egypt with about 100 women and children. They settled down near one of the city gates. [55] This opinion refers to the claim that gypsies came from Egypt, whereas other sources state that they penetrated Europe coming from Balkan during the Middle Ages and that they were roaming people who entered Western Europe disguised in pilgrimages and this way they gradually spread. [56]

Some myths also assigned gypsies to the east, especially Egypt and, as always known, everyone worked in jugglery and witchery and did roaming shows on public roads is called "Egyptian". [57]

Similarly, that's what might have recently happened here in Iraq. We heard our fathers and grandfathers and other old people calling those who are described as tricky and decisive practising what was

---

[54] Clebert, Encyclopaedia, op cit., p. 100.

[55] Greenfield, Op. Cit, p. 13

[56] Franser, Angus, De Zigeuners, Atlas-Contact, 1st edition, 1999, p.9.

[57] Clebert, Op. Cit., P 22

mentioned earlier as (Ayyaroun of Egypt) referring to whoever does things like that, and they are also named as cunnings or yobs. This kind of belief does not support the hypothesis of gypsies being originally Egyptians. [58]

Gypsies were not known in the Western world during the fifteenth century by (the Egyptians) name whereas they claimed that they came from the banks of the Nile.

Gypsies in Europe called themselves the princes of Egypt Minor. They also leaned, concerning their origin, on the prophecy of Ezekiel: (I'll disperse Egyptians among nations). In Russia, Gypsies claimed that (while they were crossing the Red Sea chased by Pharaoh, a boy and a girl incredibly survived the disaster and got married to be like Gypsies' Adam and Eve). [59]

Volkanius Benuventura believes that gypsies came from Nubia and Robert, Samuel and Voltaire share the same point of view. In addition, the American Encyclopaedia claims that gypsies came from Egypt.

Egyptian race myth has been associated with the history of gypsies till the present time (as Nahla Imam said about the gypsy issue throughout history), and what is so strange about it is that some contemporary Egyptians believed in it and boasted that they have European brothers. [60]

---

[58] Al-Hashimi, P 72

[59] Clebert, PP 22-23

[60] Imam, Nahla, Gypsy Issue Throughout History, Al-Safeer Lebanon Newspaper, 6-6-2000.

Iraq:

Jean-Paul Clébert says that there are lots of myths which, sometimes, correspond with the historical information that state they grew up and came from "between rivers" countries and ancient Asia from which they migrated to India and settled down in the Chaldean land. Another myth states that some of them migrated with Prophet Abraham from Ur to Egypt while in another myth they claimed that they built Babylon and made it their capital before being defeated by Koresh the Persian and migrated towards the west and east. In India, they met their fellows who had already migrated. Those who travelled to the west claimed that they constructed Marseille and made the Rhône River. The latest two views are different, the first one is of Father Fluorite chief of gypsies in France, who claimed that they migrated from India, while the other is of kako Judy who told a Belgian gypsiologist about it and, on the contrary, he claimed that their migration was from Chaldean land towards India. [61]

Bouderborne believes that gypsies were of Babylonian origin, they had to migrate after the destruction of their capital, while Dr Fawzi Rashid, a professor of ancient history at the College of Art of Baghdad University, wrote research entitled (Who are gypsies and what their origin is?). He concluded that gypsies came from the area surrounding Samara city (about 155 km. north of Baghdad) which was first initiated during the sixth millennium BC. To prove that the following is his evidence:

1. Gypsies' current customs and traditions are like those of the Sumerians at that time in this place among which is the dance of

---

[61] - Clebert, op. cit., PP 22-27

head and hair rotation from the right side which was a ceremony conducted by gypsy families to bring rain, when scarce, to this area (near Samara) which depends on rain. In this ceremony, four women stand facing each other on each side and do the dance, which is similar, according to Dr Rashid, to the gypsies' dance nowadays (shaking and rotating their hair). People gave them lots of money, as alms, for doing the ceremony and the dance and that made gypsy neglect agriculture, and this way their life went on.

2. Gypsy women do horoscope reading as they were doing in their homeland near Samarra. The woman was previously the chief of religious agricultural ceremonies revealing horoscopes for rulers and countries.

3. Gypsies, now, work in mining as the Sumerians did in the past. Archaeological discoveries indicate that copper mining was first known in the northern areas of Iraq, and they used copper during the same period in which they reached southern Iraq.

4. Gypsies reached Europe in the first millennium after being widespread in Asia and Africa. Most probably, the group that arrived there, previously settled down in India, therefore, western researchers emphasised that gypsies' origin is India.

5. Dr Rashid thinks that Gypsies don't look like Indians!! And that sustains his hypothesis of not being Indian.

6. The name that gypsies were given by the people of southern Iraq is Kawliya which is a corrupted form of the Sumerian word (kowli) which means (a friend), this name was given to the immigrants coming from Samarra towards the south and lived among its Sumerian people who speak the same language as theirs whereas there wasn't any animosity among them that was why they were called friends.

What sustains that truth is the slang Sabian Mandai accent which can be considered contemporary to the Sumerian language, and it calls gypsies "kowli", as a word, exists in the Sumerian language meaning "a friend". While the name (Ghajer) "Gajer", was their name before they came to the southern part of Iraq and, since they are a sparse group, they lived a grazing life mainly depending on the milk of their sheep. This means that milk was among the most important food resources. And because "milk" in Sumerian language is pronounced (Ga) while the verb "deals with" is pronounced (ger), people of areas surrounding Samarra called them "Gajer" i.e., who depend on milk as their main food whereas the first (G) turned into (gh) in Arabic and the other one into (J), this way the name became (Ghajer) in Arabic, as Dr. Rashid explained.

Therefore, as Dr Rashid said that the name "gypsy Ghajer" was used by the Egyptians rather than Iraqis, the reason behind that is that the Iraqis knew them by the name "Kawliya" or "kewliya" and there was no need to look for another name while the Egyptians the latter name and used the original name "Gajer". Sumerian language studies revealed that most of the names of tools, professions, and peoples, 6000 years ago BC and up, end in "r" like "Gager", "Summer" and "Dinker", which means "god" and the like. [62]

We think that Dr Fawzi Rashid relies on the gypsies' cultural characteristics, or some of them to be more correct, which he found some of their Sumerian equivalent ones. However, we think that cultural characteristics are acquired and changeable across time

---

[62] Rashid, Fawzi, Who Are the Gypsies, a study under publication, College of Art – Baghdad University, 1994.

and his opinion would be more accurate if he relied on physical characteristics are more stable than cultural ones.

In addition, we don't know why they do the rain dance, which is a ceremony to bring rain, when needed, to their homeland areas as he said, which are near Samarra and depend on rain. Nevertheless, in the south, there is no need for such a ceremony since the area depends on river water which is plenty and available.

Moreover, is it reasonable that they were obliged by other people, who were their friends as he said, to change their career into another one and then they gave them alms? And is it reasonable for people to be forced to accept practising a job like dancing and live on alms leaving their original job as farmers? If we suppose that they did, then why didn't they return to their previous works and jobs when justifications were gone i.e., when rain fell?

In addition, we mentioned that they had another job, which is mining. Is this job subject to rainy circumstances? Divine, religious, travelling, literature books of Arab and neighbouring countries besides Arabic poetry, never talk about gypsies in this area or what looked like their lifestyle since gypsy life always tempts poets' tramps and the like.

Concerning gypsies' name "Kawliya", (the name they are known by in Iraq, corrupted into Kawawla in Kuwait and the Gulf region) we have reached a different conclusion from that of Dr Rashid, the opinion that we may tend to can be applied to Indian tribes whose some women practice sex work and dancing as a religious service for religious men and for money for whoever wants sexual pleasure, among them were in King Chola temple. They related themselves to King Chola to honour and glorify them and what Will Durant mentioned in the part of India in his famous book "The Story of Civilization", can sustain this opinion. This opinion refutes what was common about Dr Mustafa Jawad's hypothesis which assumes that gypsies' name came from Kabul, the capital of Afghanistan because they passed it, but the name was changed over time. [63] This research sustains our opinion besides the probability that they belong to India rather than any other country.

India

Being related to India was unknown until the nineteenth century, but an article appeared in Vein newspaper on November the sixth 1763 signed by Captain Szekely von Doba, revealed this strange discovery; a young Hungarian man named Stephen Vali, who was studying theology in Leiden University in Holland, met three Indian students from Malabar coast and noticed that these students' language was similar to Hungarian language and wrote down about a thousand of their words. When he returned home, he showed these words to the gypsies, and he found out that they easily explained them. [64]

Gypsiologists analysed these words, and their meanings and linguists tracked them and other linguistic traces since it was necessary to track these gypsy-like human groups within the huge population of India. They found gypsy-like groups in India and compared them according to the letter, among them were Handi Vokey tribes who were beggars

---

[63]   See: Jawad, Mustafa, Gypsies in Arab Resources, Al-Arabi magazine, Kuwait, issue no. 126, May 1969.

[64]   - Imam, Op Cit.

and swindlers, Kami who were makers and blacksmiths from Nepal, Kasira or Kasara who worked in casting tin and were metal makers in India, Korava from Tamil area were horoscope readers, swindlers and thieves, Lohar who were makers from the north, Nat who were singers, dancers and robe players, in addition to Tatera, Kanjar, Dom and Asora, Lori and Gazia tribes. (Ghawazi gypsies in Egypt may belong to the latter tribe). But researchers were only attracted by Dom. So, this discovery came late in Europe, but in the Middle East, it's well known in Arab or Persian sources for several centuries. This could be the same in neighbouring countries like Turkey or others.

Persian poet Ferdowsi (about a thousand-year AD) claimed, in his book "Shah Nameh", that in 420 AD, Bahram Gur, a Sassanid ruler who ruled from 266 to 461 AD, noticed that his people were eager to delight, so he looked for means by which he could raise his morale. He sent a diplomatic delegation to Shankal, the king of Mekboria and the Mehraja of India, asking him to choose some of his people who were able to lessen life burdens and spread joy and delight among his people since they worked hard and lived in poverty, and then send them to Persia. As a response, Bahram Gur got twelve thousand women and men roaming as singers. He allocated a piece of land for them in which they could live and work, and so they could entertain his people for free.

By the end of their first year there, they abandoned agriculture and consumed all the grains and became without any source of living. That made Bahram angry with them and ordered them to confiscate their donkeys as well as their musical instruments and make them roam across the country as roaming singers. These people, who were known as the Lor, began to roam all over the world as jobseekers taking with them their dogs and foxes. They were stealing day and night during their roaming. This event was chronicled by the Persian Hamza Al-Esfahani in 940 AD. Sir Henry Pottinger also chronicled this incident in his book (Journeys to India and Baluchistan), published in 1816.

Researchers emphasised the relationship between the Dom or Lum group, they were called Dom in Syria and Iran, and they called themselves Rom in Europe. Cole Blouch mentioned that the Dom tribe was well known in India for a long time whereas in the Persian dictionary (Ferhank Anndraj) "Kawly" is a synonym for Lore which was used to call an Indian group of people.))))

He also mentioned that King Shahpoor brought thousands of those people from Kabul to Shahpoor in Khuzestan, men were builders while their women danced, sang and drank besides sleeping with men at night. [65]

In old Arabic sources, Father Anstas Mary Al-Karmali and Dr. Mustafa Jawad both agreed that Zutt and Kawliya belong to India being their original homeland. Other old Arabic sources emphasised on Gypsies' race like Al-Balathery in his book "Futooh Al-Buldan" mentioning their events during Al-Mamoon era, and Abul-Hassan Al-Saudi in his book "Al-Tanbeeh wa Al-Ishraq", Al-Fayrooz Abadi, Ibn Al-Mathoor in his book "Lissan Al-Arab" and Ibn Al-Atheer in his book "Al-Kamil fi AL-Tareekh" beside modern Arabic sources like Islamic Encyclopaedia all agreed on this idea. [66]

---

[65] - Ibid, P. 35
[66] -Al-Hadithi, op. cit., P. 16

The gypsy researcher Rajko Đurić, the author of "Gypsies' journey across the World", believes that most researchers agree that gypsy first went to Iran after leaving India which means that India was their homeland. [67]

Gypsiologists could not agree on a specific date for gypsies' immigration from India. And so, it is unreasonable and illogical to think that gypsies suddenly spread in the East. But 1000 AD could be a suitable year for that immigration which continues till this day. [68]

Among other opinions is that their language and complexion indicate that they came from India (Jareedat Al-Iraq) and that they belonged to the Jit people who are available in India and Pakistan. Arabs knew these people before Islam and Arabicized the name to become Zutt. Dutch orientalist de Goeje was the most important researcher who promote this theory (died in 1909) in his book "Gypsies' immigration across Asia" in which he depended on Arabic and Persian sources. [69]

Conclusion:

After reviewing previous opinions and hypotheses, we believe that the myth-based opinions toggled that gypsies' origin is the Middle East (Egypt, Palestine or Iraq) while other opinions rely on congenital and cultural similarities to identify their origin to be either India or Egypt. Some other opinions depend on the place they came from or their different names to identify their origin.

---

[67] - Đurić, op. cit., P.16
[68] - Clebert, op. cit., P.41
[69] Imam, op. cit.

Since gypsies had bad behaviours, they tended to change their names and origins or attribute themselves to tribes or areas of good reputation and origin.

The most preponderant opinions are those which suggest India to be their origin for the following reasons:

1. Cultural similarities of traditions, professions, and language are extremely similar despite the time gap between the time they left India and nowadays.
2. Physical similarity (physical features like complexion, hair, contours of the face, size of skull ...... etc.) with Indian tribes and groups of people, and this was proved by physical anthropologists' efforts.
3. Old sources agreed, especially the Middle Eastern ones like those of the Arab homeland and Iran, on the Indian origin of gypsies.
4. It is not reasonable that gypsy groups appeared in the Islamic and Arab communities after Islam, if these groups were present before Islam, Islamic rules wouldn't allow their existence since they did not represent a heavenly religion or a specified nationality.

Because of the weakness of other hypotheses, the gypsies' Indian origin hypothesis is the most probable one because of its strength and became an axiom for gypsiologist taking into consideration that the scientific method required questioning which leads to continuous research and discussing any new thought might appear in the scientific field.

Common Gypsies' Characteristics in the World:

Since most of the opinions agree that all gypsies belong to a united origin, there must be common characteristics they share by which they are easily distinguished from others. These characteristics made them a distinct subculture within the prevailing culture and that led to the emergence of intellectual movements or what is called (the Gypsy Emission Movement) or (the National Awakening of Gypsies) which appeared in the mid-nineteenth century, the same time when Emancipation Act for gypsy slaves was announced in Romania which included a quarter of a million gypsies. Gypsy slaves' uprising in 1878 was considered a big turning point for gypsies; it was the first time that gypsies tried to form on a new basis. When Joseph Reinhardt called gypsy representatives from Italy, Spain, and Russia to a meeting near Stuttgart (Germany) to agree on establishing an organisation that look after gypsies' interests.

In 1879, gypsies tried to hold a meeting in Kewal village in Hungary, but the authorities there prevented them. In May 1891, George Smith went to the English Parliament asking for their intervention with the government in solving the gypsies' problems in England and the gypsy statement in Bulgaria belongs to that time.

In 1900, the first gypsy dream became true when the gypsy school was opened in Sofia although it didn't continue long because it was closed shortly after the beginning of October socialist revolution.

In Russia, there were several attempts to do a similar act for the interest of gypsies until the end of the 1920s when suddenly all doors opened to form gypsy organisations. The Russian Gypsy Union was established, magazines and radio programs were issued in gypsy language, books were published, and a gypsy theatre was opened.

In Romania, gypsy awakening took a fundamental form since about two million gypsies live there which is considered the largest gathering of gypsies in eastern Europe. At the beginning of the 30s, Gregory Nikolsky activated the call for establishing a global organisation for gypsies and he succeeded in holding a conference for gypsy representatives in Europe in Bucharest in November 1933. In that conference, the call to form a national state for gypsies emerged, either in the original homeland or in northern Africa which meant at the expense of Arabs.

In Hungary, The Union of Gypsies was formed in 1958 than similar organisations were established in the rest of countries like (Western) Germany, Spain, Finland, Sweden, France.... etc.

In 1971, the first global conference for gypsies was held in London which resulted in establishing the global organisation of gypsies and choosing a flag and a united anthem for gypsies. The first connection with the homeland was conducted through the Indian embassy in London. In 1983, gypsies achieved another victory when De Remos Ramirez-Heredia, presidential member of the Global Organisation of Gypsies, won in the Spanish elections for the European Council and that enabled him to raise the issue of gypsies' rights and their social conditions in some European countries more than once. [70]

In 1937, the Baghdadi Arab World newspaper wrote the following item of news under the title "King of Gypsies in Poland":

---

[70] Đurić, op. cit., PP. 187-188.

A coronation ceremony for the Polish gypsy king has been held recently in the military games square near Warsaw after being elected by 30 Gypsy notables. He was seen sitting on his throne wearing official clothes, his name is Janusz Kwiek. The end of the item of news. [71]

In similar news, Al Shabab TV from Darul-Salam in Baghdad broadcasted at the end of 1993 a video report about crowning the gypsy king in Spain. The king appeared in royal customs riding a fancy car surrounded by a large retinue whereas some Spanish officials and foreign diplomats attended the ceremony. [72]

All that confirmed gypsies' orientation towards unity and common sense and that sustained inevitability of their common origin. Different studies in the world confirmed the huge affinity and similarity among gypsy groups. Clot Beck described Egyptian gypsies saying (Gypsies can be distinguished from others by their mien, their complexion is darker than that of the Egyptians and their language is different from Arabic. Despite claiming to be Muslims, they do not do any of Islam's duties, roaming from town to town and from village to another altogether or individually. Men work in juggling and tricks. While women can be distinguished by their strange clothes, they work in horoscope reading. [73]

---

[71] - Baghdadi Arab World Newspaper, Baghdad, issue no. 3977 on Aug. 22nd, 1937.
[72] - Al-Shabab TV, Baghdad, 9pm news of April 22nd, 1993.
[73] Al-Far, Ali Islam, Dictionary of Sociology, 1st edition, Egyptian Encyclopaedia, El Maarif House, Egypt, 1978, P.153.

Al-Shabab Magazine in Egypt mentioned the following:

'They have common features like dark skin, black hair, and shiny eyes, they roam from one place to another and when they arrive in villages, they claim to belong to big, effective families to be allowed to enter. They have their own language.... Etc'. [74]

Manchip White wrote describing native gypsies in India:

(They are tall and have limbs; their skin is darker than others anywhere. Their women are nicer, with a wide face which are affected by the sun to become brown, their eyes are shiny, and their hair is long and black. They work as jugglers, roaming musicians raising cattle. Women are acrobats, dancers and they work in the circus. Women also work in nursing, horoscope reading and doing tattoos. Their children are naked and dirty. They eat castrated bullocks and dead horses due to diseases. [75]

Horacio Roney wrote about some gypsy Indian tribes' habits especially marriage habits saying. There is no coercion in marriage and their passions and after marriage; the wife becomes, in general, loyal to her husband. Wedding parties are united; the bride comes to his fiancée's cottage asking for her hand. She refuses with mockery, but she soon softens her opinion when she finds him too headstrong to be refused, then he abandons her, but they ask him to treat her well.

---

[74] Mansoor, Nadia, Gypsies in Egypt, Al-Shabab Magazine Egypt, 1989.
[75] - White, Op. Cit, P. 64.

He tattoos her forehead and conducts a banquet of wines and parties that cost them a lot. [76]

Dr Fawzi Rashid summarized some of gypsy features as the following: [77]
1. Music, singing, dancing and roaming theatre.
2. Horoscope reading, especially their women.
3. Living in carts and tents (continuous roaming).
4. Working in witchcraft.
5. Working in the metal industry (iron, bronze and gold).
6. Being illiterate.
7. They hate water and don't often take showers.

In Webster's dictionary, gypsies are described as:

'They live roaming, homeless and in Bedouin life; their women are deceptive. They have got yellow complexion and black hair. They are originally Indian, and they are a global phenomenon. Their language is called Romani'. [78]

Most of these features are almost the same in all gypsies in the world. Gypsies in Iraq share lots of these features. Generally, gypsies all over the world share the following:
1. Continuous travelling.
2. Having their language.
3. Indian origin.

---

76 Roney, Horacio, The wild tribes of India, B. R. Publishing, Cooperation, Delhi, 1974, P.P. 12-13.
77 Rashid, op. cit., PP. 1-6.
78 Webster, Op. Cit, P. 678.

4. Physical appearance (bronze colour, black soft straight hair and bright almond-like eyes).
5. Their crafts are (blacksmith, circus, horoscope reading, music and dancing).

Gypsies and Holocaust:

Holocaust, as a word, is a term used to describe the Nazi-organised government campaigns conducted by the German government and some of its allies for persecution and ethnic cleansing against Jews in Europe during World War II. This word is derived from the Greek word holókauston, ὁλόκαυστον which means "to burn sacrifices presented to the Creator of the universe". In the nineteenth century, this word was used to describe huge catastrophes or tragedies. The first time "holocaust" was used to describe how Hitler treated Jews was in 1942, but it didn't spread widely enough until the 1950s. In the 1970s, the word was exclusively used to refer to the genocide against Jews by the German authorities during the Nazi Party's reign under the command of Hitler. Jews themselves used the word האישׁ, which is mentioned in the Torah and means "catastrophe", instead of "holocaust". [79]

"Holocaust" can be systematically described as an organised, well-thought-out and fully industrially executed process in which six million European Jews were murdered. In addition, many Roma, LGBTQ+ individuals, and others deemed 'unwanted' or 'unworthy

---

[79] - Wikipedia Free Encyclopaedia on the Internet, ar.wikipedia.org, March 10th, 2007.

of life' by the Nazis were also murdered. People, in a very brutal scheme, were exploited, tortured, humiliated, and murdered in death factories and concentration camps. Before the operations of killing, there were racial media campaigns spreading Anti-Semitic ideas and the Jews were deprived of their civil rights besides isolating them and confiscating their properties. Holocaust operations were not restricted to government agencies only, other groups from the army and different industrial, banking, scientific and medical organisations took part in them. [80]

However, gypsies were among the victims of the Nazis and their extreme acts especially human incinerators which were known as the Holocaust. But the light was always shed on the Jewish victims or the Jewish themselves as victims.

Unfortunately, gypsies were either forgotten or ignored they were victims of those brutal crimes. Few of us know that the Nazis led them along with the Jewish to the incinerators and burned about 650,000 of them during the war. While the world was and still, day after day, concerned about the holocaust of the Jews and pay compensations of billions to them and Israel, no one pays the gypsies any kind of compensation for what happened to them and what they had lost of their families. What is harder than all that is that people know nothing about the disaster, and nothing is said about it in the media. [81]

---

[80] Facts about Germany web site, http://www.tatsachen-ueber-deutschland.de/ar/
history/content/glossary03.html?type=1&tx_a21glossary%5Buid%5D=1467&tx_
a21glossary%5Bback%5D=151&cHash=e2cc4b7507.

[81] - Al-Qashtini, Khalid, The Forgotten Holocaust, an article published in The Middle East newspaper in London, issue no. 8229, June 9th, 2001.

The numbers of gypsies' genocide victims and the motives behind it vary and differ according to gypsiologist and historians of the holocaust. Yehuda Bauer, a Holocaust historian, for an instance, confirms that the murder of gypsies was different from that of the Jews. Since gypsies were not Jewish, it was unnecessary to exterminate them. But with the beginning of Soviet invasion in Jun 1941, repression and torture against gypsies began to turn into genocide in Poland and Russia and Balkan region accusing them of being spies. Thus, 250,000 or more were killed. [82]

Animosity against gypsies is not the result of a specific era but it is renewed over time and places due to the nature of gypsies' life which is characterized by continuous roaming and their professions which, most of the time, disturb peoples they live with. But in Germany, animosity mixed with ethnic ideology which followed certain approaches to deal with other ethnicities.

Exterminating gypsies was listed in the agenda of Nazi Germany. Since 1899, Bavarian police had a special department for gypsy affairs which was receiving copies of decisions of courts which were responsible for deciding on violations committed by gypsies. In 1929, this department turned into a national centre whose headquarters was in Munich and since then, gypsies were prevented from locomotion without police permission. In addition, jobless gypsies over 16 years old were obliged to work for two years in one of the rehabilitation centres. And since 1933, which was the year Hitler reached power, these restrictions became more severe and strict. Gypsies with no

---

[82] Fonisca, Isabel, Gypsies' Biography, a summary review published in Al Zawraa web site, http://www.alzawraa.net/home/index.php?option=com_content&task=view&id=6902&Itemid=232، 10-3-2007.

German nationality were expelled while the rest were put in detention centres claiming that they were "unsocial". [83]

Since gypsies' life is characterized by continuous travelling, they do not prefer working in permanent jobs or professions that require spatial stabilization in addition to their lack of education and skills. Moreover, this feature weakens their moral commitment due to anonymity besides their ignorance about these things. Depending upon that, violations, perversions, and crimes are more often among them.

And so, gypsies are always subject to suspicion and distrust and often to severity as we found in the regulations that Germany applied at that time. Then the interest and caution from gypsies tended to be scientific "to exterminate them", as it seemed, they concentrated on studying the "gypsies' ethnic characteristics", Dr Hans Globke, who associated with legislating Nuremberg laws in 1936, announced that the blood in gypsies' veins was "foreign". Hans F. Guenther classified them as an independent category representing an undefined ethnic mixture (as he couldn't deny their Aryan origin). Gypsies' ethnic characteristics were so important that they could be suitable to be subject for a PhD thesis. Among things that Eva Justin, Dr Ritter's assistant in ethnic research at the Ministry of Health when she discussed her thesis, was that gypsy blood "represents a grave danger on the purity of the German race". Notice here how science was oriented to serve extreme ideological purposes.

---

[83]   El-Messiri, Abdel-Wahab, Jews, Judaism and Zionism, Nazi extermination against gypsies, Gypsies Nazi Extermination of‹ http://www.elmessiri.com/Zionism/jewish/ENCYCLOPID/START/..%5CMG2%5CGZ4%5CBA4%5CMD1111. HTM‹ 11-3-2007.

Later, gypsies were criminalized because of the standards that were adopted at that time when, on December 14th, 1936, a resolution was issued to consider gypsies as "criminals who are habitual to criminality". By the end of 1937 and through 1938, campaigns of arrests were launched against gypsies and detained in an allocated part of the Bocholt detention centre. Dead lists of lots of concentration camps, involved gypsy names like: Natzweiler, Malthouse, Flossenburg, Justin and Dautmergen. In Ravensbrück, lots of Gypsy women were victims of experiments conducted by the physicians of the Hitlerite military police "SS". Himmler ordered to classify gypsies into the following groups: pure gypsy (Z), mulatto dominated by gypsy race (+ZM), mulatto dominated by Aryan race (-ZM) and mulatto in which gypsy and Aryan races are equal (ZM). [84]

Acts like those look funny nowadays especially when adopted by governmental agencies although launched by scientific establishments.

It is hard to estimate how many gypsies were living in Europe before World War II and how many were killed in it. The historian Raul Hilberg estimates the number of gypsies in Germany before they were as 34,000; but the number of who survived after it is unknown. Execution teams reports revealed that the number of gypsy victims in Russia, Ukraine and Qurum reached 300,000 while Yugoslav authorities estimate murdered gypsies as 28,000 in Serbia alone. In Poland, it is hard to estimate the number of victims there although the historian Tetenbaum confirms that the gypsy people lost at least 500,000 fellows despite knowing that gypsy people are deep-rooted and prolific (unlike Jews). Anyway, and even when rates were different,

---

[84]   Ibid.

the rate of gypsies who were exterminated (to their total number) is more than that of the Jews. [85]

The French Jewish historian George Whirl estimated those who were killed by gas or other means or tortured to death or famine or disease in the Auschwitz camp as bout 1.4 million people. According to this estimation, 1.35 million of them were Jews, 38000 Polish, 20000 gypsies, and 12000 Soviet prisoners of war, in addition to 150000 Polish were imprisoned in Auschwitz camps and then transported to other places where many of them, not most of them, died. [86]

What we would like to clarify here in this research, about gypsies and the Holocaust, is that these awful acts stroke gypsies to become another disaster which could be added to those that they already had. And to remind us of that History, to some extent, ignored this crime and light was shed only on the Jews as victims of those brutal acts.

---

[85] Ibid.
[86] Iranian Al-Wifaq Newspaper, The Historians of the Holocaust and exaggeration in numbers, no. 2274, March 11th, 2004.

Chapter Three

Gypsies of Iraq

Settlement locations

Demographic aspects

Gypsies in Kamaliya neighbourhood in Baghdad

Gypsies in Fawwar village in Diwaniyah

Gypsies of Iraq:

Most of the opinions nearly agreed that gypsy origin is from India and migrated towards the north and west, in terms of tribal waves which we talked about in a previous chapter. Concerning their arrival to Iraq, Dr Mustafa Jawad mentioned that the "Zutt" is the oldest name for Gypsies in Iraq. They were recognized for the first time in Iraq during the reign of Hajaj Ben Yousif Al-Thaqafi, governor of Iraq, in early the seventh century A.D. (Go back to the section of Gypsy names, the Zutt).

Even if we assume that they were the first gypsy groups to arrive in the region and Iraq and that migrations had followed in series, where are the Zutt among those who are available now?

And why don't they hold their name or history?

There is no doubt that there had been other waves of migration followed one after the other, and each held a different name, among which is "Kawliya", their name in Iraq now (Go back to names section). Gypsies, until the early 1980s, were considered foreigners and strangers by the modern Iraqi state since its establishment in 1921. [87]

Gypsies in Iraq are characterized by certain features that make them a sub-culture which is different from the wider community culture, among these features are:

---

[87] Revise Taha Al-Hadithi, Gypsies and Qarach in Iraq.

1. Physical features: like their yellowish brown or coppery complexion, fine dark black hair, black eyes, and medium height, although admixture effects (Gypsisation) can still be seen now.
2. Ethnic features: their Indian origin, physical features, culture, and their language approve that.
3. Some living features: like practising some economic careers which the Iraqi community generally doesn't.
4. Some cultural features: through their deeds which are against the common traditions and customs of the Iraqi community.

Map 1: Administrative map/provinces

Gypsy settlements' locations in Iraq:

Gypsy settlements' locations in Iraq:

Gypsies gather in populated settlements lie in big cities' suburbs and that is exactly what they need for their jobs such as constant contact with people and safe places near cities. However, most of their gatherings did not settle due to continuous immigration.

The government associated with settling them down by either dedicating lots or building houses for them.

The following are the most important locations that are inhabited by gypsies in Iraq (see map no.1):

1. Gypsy gathering in Hamam Al-Alil: they are a group of houses built during the 1980s by the government as homes for some gypsies, they lie in the Hammam Al-Alil sub-district in Mosul province.

2. Gypsies' camps in Taza sub-district: which is a camp of about 30 tents (as first established during the end of the 1980s of the twentieth century) distributed in two rows while the gypsy local sheikh's tent lies in the middle. This area administratively belongs to Kirkuk province in the north of Iraq.

3. The gypsy area in Abu-Ghraib: they inhabited there during the 1970s of the last centuries, it is isolated from the local community, and it administratively belongs to the Abu-Ghraib district in Baghdad's western suburbs.

4. Gypsy area in Kamaliya: it is one of the inhabited neighbourhoods which lie in Bagdad's eastern suburbs, and it is the sample for this thesis.

5. Gypsy area in Fawar: it is the inhabited village for gypsies lying near Diwaniyah city (centre of Qadisiya province) about 10 Km. to the north, this village is the other sample for this thesis.

6. Gypsy area in Kanaan sub-district: administratively, it belongs to Diyala province; gypsies settled there at the end of 1970s of the last century, and it was characterized by stability.

7. Gypsy area in Al-Khudr: it lies in Al-Khudr district which is administratively part of Al-Muthanna (Samawa) province. It was first inhabited by gypsies early in the 1980s after being displaced and moved from the Al-Sharaka area, which is approximately far from the district centre, in the west of the same province.

8. Gypsy area in Al-Shomali: it lies near to Al-Shomali district of Babil province. They inhabited the area during the middle of the 1980s.

9. Gypsy area in Al-Shatra: it lies in Bani Zaid in the Al-Shatra district which is part of Thi-Qar province (Al-Nasiriyah). Gypsies moved there after being evacuated from their previous settlement near Al-Fajr sub-district in the same province.

10. There are some residents near gypsies in some big cities like Basra, which are undiagnosed by the government or common people, sometimes, except some of their customers who often come to them.

11. Some gypsy families are still moving like Bedouins, especially in the north of Nainava and towns nearby Aljazeera desert-like Al-Shirqat, Mosul, and Haweeja.

Population of Gypsies of Iraq:

There is no precise population census for gypsies because they, previously, were continuously moving, and they never gave reliable data and statistics because they fear these things.

Until shortly before the fall of the ex-regime, there were reasonable population censuses for gypsies who were considered Iraqis. These censuses, usually, do not distinguish who is gypsy from who is not, but they depend on their residential gatherings. Therefore, gypsies who live solo in the city, for instance, or outside villages and gypsy neighbourhoods could not be verified or distinguished, especially after getting Iraqi citizenship. Being so, they are nearly equal to others in legal and civil obligations among which is sending their sons to military service.

In a report from United Nations Office for Humanitarian Affairs on March 3rd, 2005, posted on "Relief Web" internet site: "There is no official total population statistics for gypsies in Iraq, but Sheikh of gypsy tribes estimate the number to be over that 60,000 and 11,000 of them are in Diwaniyah" [88] The Region's homepage Philly.com also estimate gypsy's population to be 50,000.

But there is no possibility to verify these estimations, especially within the current circumstances in Iraq. There are some previous estimations, we present the best of them which is that of Dr Taha Al-Hadithi which includes a table of estimations for gypsy's and Qarach's population until 2000.

---

[88] http://www.philly.com/mld/philly/news/11823843.htm available at: 03/01/2006.

The population of gypsies in Iraq is much bigger than these estimations because gypsies were known to be careful, elusive and afraid of giving correct information and also for the constant increase in their numbers since non-gypsy people tend to become gypsies (gypsy making) through resettlement, work, or marriage, especially those women who want to live a gypsy life or been drawn to work with them and it is hard for them to go back to their lives mainly for social considerations.

Usually, there are two types of living and settlement in gypsy areas in Iraq, more particularly gypsies in Kamaliya which are considered a distinguished style of settlement. This style has certain features, the most important of which is neighbouring (Arabs), as gypsies use to call them, who are non-gypsy people and that offer direct contact with them and offers other basic services. Other settlements are completely different in that they are just isolated villages and are almost denied services. We will have a look at Kamaliya as a sample and Fawwar in Qadisiya (Diwaniyah) as another sample for gypsies in south-central Iraq.

Table-1 shows number of gypsies and Qarch according to rates of general births and deaths in 1976.

	Numbers of families	Total families' members	Births	General rate of births in thousandth	Deaths	General rate of deaths in thousands	Rate of growth	Estimation for their number in 1987	Their estimated number in 2000
Gypsies	1069	5569	210	37.7	49	8.8	28.9	7404	10510
Qarach	465	2256	106	46.98	28	12.41	34.57	3680	5613
Total	1561	7825	316	42.34	77	10.6	31.7	11084	16123

The numbers of gypsies in Iraq are much higher than these estimates, as fear, caution and evasion are known about gypsies in giving correct information, in addition to the continuous increase in their numbers due to the process (gypsy making) that happens to numbers of non-gypsy people through settlement, work, integration or intermarriage with them, especially women who want to live as gypsies or are lured to work in their midst and it is difficult for them to return for primarily social considerations.

There are usually two types of habitation or settlement in the gypsy areas of Iraq. In particular, the residence of gypsies in Kamaliya area of Baghdad can be distinguished as a form of distinct settlement of gypsies. This is characterized by certain features, perhaps the most important of which is the adjacent housing with (Arabs), who are non-gypsies, as called by the gypsies, and the results of direct contact with them. This is in addition to the availability of other basic services. As for the other settlement areas, they are completely different in that they are isolated villages that are almost deprived of most of these services. Below we will see both Kamaliya sample and another corresponding samples, which is the gypsy area in Fawwar in the province of Qadisiya (Diwaniyah) in south-central Iraq.

Gypsy area in Kamaliya:

This area is characterized by the following:
a. It is the oldest stable gathering of gypsies in Iraq; it has been inhabited since 1958.
b. It is the only inhabited area which is open to non-gypsy gatherings, and it is known for direct neighbouring relationships.

c. It is the most changeable gypsy area because of its location in Baghdad.

d. It is the most active gypsy area and offers job opportunities for gypsies because of its location.

Gypsies live in the neighbourhood no. 757 and some residents in the neighbourhood no. 756 all within Kamaliya which holds a population of about 20,000.

Administratively, Kamaliya is part of the Baghdad Al-Jadida sub-district to the north within the capital Baghdad. Gypsies are about 2400 in population distributed among 260 families living in 217 houses. [89] They started living in this area in 1958, they were 1019 in population at the time and distributed among 174 families. [90]

At that time, their houses were just huts or houses of reeds and nobody neighbours them because the area was not inhabited at that time. Now, their location controls the entrance to Kamaliya and Al-Fudiliyah on the side of the main street (old Diyala Road) and this location is also near the main marketplace there.

The nature of the area is purely urban, and it is affected, to some extent, by the capital Baghdad. Its houses indicate the high standards of living of many gypsies there and some of these houses are so sophisticated and emulate homes in some classy neighbourhoods in Baghdad.

---

[89]   Al-Mukhtar Al-Mahala records in 1994
[90]   Al-Hadithi, Op. Cit, p. 50.

Services provided:
This area has lots of services like other Baghdad neighbourhoods, among which are:
1. Water and electricity services.
2. Phone services.
3. Schools of all levels (associated with the rest of the people there)
4. Paved streets, although internal streets are in bad shape.

Map 2: The location of each of the study areas (Kamaliya and Fawwar).

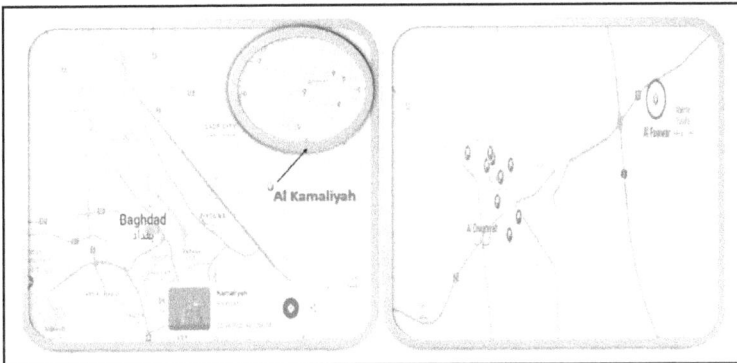

Gypsy area of Fawwar:

The Gypsy area in Fawwar, unlike Kamaliya, did not change because they did not have direct contact with people since their village is isolated from other neighbourhoods and villages in the province. Although its activity has diminished if not finished because of the changes referred to, this area has the following features:
a) It is also one of the oldest gypsy gatherings, (they started to settle in this area in 1963 and inhabited it in 1973).

b) It is an isolated area from other neighbourhoods, and it is like other gypsy gatherings in Iraq.

c) It suffers from many problems; the lack of public services is the most important one.

Fawwar lies in a relatively conservative area (Qadisiya province), being so, it differs from Baghdad. Moreover, it is near holy shrines in Najaf, Kufa, and Karbala.

Fawwar is a sort of isolated village which is 12 km away to the northeast of Diwaniyah at the end of a 2 km branch road starting from the main road that links Diwaniyah and Afak passing by Al Jamiyya village for the same distance. Fawwar lies in lot 3 and part of lot 2 of territory 22 which is called (Abu-Tarareed). (See Map no. 4). Its area is about 24 acres. Gypsies started to settle down since 1963 and they have settled down there since 1970, they built 50 houses of reed and clay. Their Sheikh at the time was Bezaiea Taghi.

Up to now, these houses are not their personal property and the same amount has been deducted from them for the interest of the governmental properties.[91]

Their population reached 2500 in 1987 and their total buildings number 292 according to the general population census of Iraq.[92] There are circa 226 families occupying 220 houses.[93]

---

[91]   Diwaniyah mayor office.

[92]   Census directorate of Qadisiya province.

[93]   Ibid.

This village is characterized by urban features that appeared clearly in their inhabitancy nature along with some activities despite their abandonment of country values.

They were offered the following services:
1. Electricity
2. A paved 2 km road linking the village with Al-Jamiyya village and the Diwaniyah-Afak Road.
3. One primary school called "Al-Islah" was established in 1987. It is administratively belonging to the mayor's office of Diwaniyah district 180 km. to the south of Baghdad.

We may notice here that this village lacks other basic services such as drinking water, phone landlines, paving its internal roads or any other services like its equivalent in Kamaliya for instance.

Chapter Four

Kinship and Marriage in the gypsy Community

Kinship System

Kinship

Marriage in the gypsy community

Household in the gypsy community

Woman as a bread owner in gypsy community

Marriage

Marriage ceremonies

Kinship System

It is an important pillar in the social structure of any society and an important aspect that cannot be ignored in anthropological studies, especially those dealing with the study of primitive, Tribal, semi-rural and even urban societies in developing countries.

''Kinship system is based on blood and marriage relations, the two main axes of the family system and the marriage system''. [94]

By blood ties, we mean here either a biological parent-child or an adoption relationship with their children or the supposed kinship among the sons of the kinship unit.

Kinship:

There are several types of kinship relations: [95]
1. Marital relationship.
2. Direct relationship among the nuclear family members and the rest of the family.
3. A relationship between the nuclear family and the rest of the relatives.

And there are three kinship degrees:
1. The central kinship includes the individual's parents, brothers and sisters, husbands, sons, and daughters in the nuclear family.

---

94 Al Bayyati Aladdin, Ilmulijtimaa Bein Alnadhariya wal Tatbiq, Dar Attarbiya, Baghdad, 1975, P. 374.
95 Al Ruaishidi, Saadi Faidhi, Introduction to Anthropology, Higher Educations Presses, Mosul, 1989, p99.

2. Second-degree relatives, represented by the brothers of the husband and wife.
3. Third-degree relatives, as secondary relatives, are usually nephews of the husband and wife.

As for the kinship units or kinship groups, they are:
1. The nuclear family, or what we call the family (see the subject of the family in this book), is a group consisting of spouses and their unmarried sons.
2. Extended nuclear family: It consists of either a polygamous family or a family in which there is polygamy in addition to children.
3. A shared family consists of two or more nuclear families linked in the father's or mother's line. Its base is shared residence, and they have joint economic and social commitments.
4. The house or progeny: It is a kinship unit consisting of a group of families descended from a common ancestor and spanning about four or five generations. Sometimes they may live together in one area.
5. lineage: It is a group of houses or progenies descended from one common grandfather or ancestor, and it spans seven or eight generations.
6. Clan: It is a group of lineage descended from a typical grandfather or ancestor and extends to about twelve generations.
7. Tribe: It is the broadest kinship unit. It consists of a group of clans descended from a common ancestor and extends to about twenty generations.

The main kinship unit here for the gypsies is the family, from which the individual's commitments begin and in which he receives the principles of socialization. He sees the light of the life that his community lives, after which the commitments to other kinship units are graded to a lesser extent.

The system of progeny and ancestry for the gypsy community is parental, through males (paternal), and they form a tourniquet kinship by the common proverb (me and my brother against my cousin and me and my cousin against the stranger). Thus, the relationship with convergence is drawn according to their grades.

The common complex family is the dominant model in the gypsy society because of the nature of their living life that requires them to gather in places dedicated to them, and according to the nature of their careers that contradicts the values of a totalitarian society (the dominant culture).

This housing congestion applies to the gypsy area of Kamaliya because the area is surrounded by Arab (not gypsy) homes. The expansion of their residential area has thus receded, which is why the rental prices of housing in the area increased.

The nature of their professions also requires a force of men that protects the family from customer abuses or that deals with the situation in favour of the family even in their assault or defrauding customers.

Power in the gypsy family belongs to the father, although the status of women is high because they are the main source of income for the family through the professions they practice.

What confirms the high status of women is that the family prefers that their baby be a female rather than a male, and that's due to the same reason above.

But in inheritance cases, the son has great power and has the lion's share, and he inherits his father in much of the money and status he leaves. The distribution of money is done in the Islamic way. In Islamic law, inheritance is distributed as it is known to be for the male having the share of two females. This is not so much a commitment to Islamic law as it is the power of men over women at the right opportunity while the status and appreciation of women is merely temporary and dependent on their giving. As a piece of evidence for that, once a woman in a gypsy society reaches an undesirable age by customers or is of a low beauty level or becomes disabled, she will be neglected and become a somewhat undesirable person even in her family.

This confirms that the status of the individual here depends on teir economic role.

Guy Young of the American University in Washington points out the conclusion of his research (Gender inequality and industrial development: The household connection) similarly saying that: "Early research based on generation and gender suggests that there are many differences based on material basis among family members and this gap and disagreement must be related to the type of work and its command as well as the intellectual conflict about women's family subordination." [96]

---

[96] Young, Gay, Gender Inequalities and Industrial Development, Journal of comparative family studies, vol. XXIV, No. 1, spring 1993, p. 1.

The status based on material basis applies to relatives residing with the family as well, as the status of the uncle, grandfather, aunt or son-in-law residing with the family (al-Ka'idi-al-Qa'idi), rises and his/her word is heard and he/she has an important role in making the decision of the captives when he is a person who spends (productive and breadwinner) of this family.

Reciprocal theory interpretation can be applied to these things, and that is what **George Homans** came up with saying that "the explicit and clear secret of human exchange is to offer others a behaviour that is more valuable to them than its cost to you, and to obtain from him a behaviour that is more valuable to you than its cost to them." [97]

In general, the situation of the gypsy family in this regard is almost identical and indeed close to that of the Iraqi family and the rural family in terms of the status of women and their role in formulating family decision-making. [98]

In his research in this regard, Dr Qais Al-Nouri believes that "the immediate situation of the Iraqi rural family in terms of taking decisions goes a long way to represent urban ways of thinking and performing. We admit here that there is some ambiguity related to the existence of endless issues and issues related to a transitional phase". [99]

---

[97] Zeitlin, Irving, The Contemporary Theory of Sociology, translated by Mahmoud Oda and Ibrahim Othman, printed by Thatulsalasil press, Kuwait, 1986, p 122.

[98] See Saadi Al Ruaishidi, Arab Homeland Anthropology, High Education Presses, Mosul, 1990, p 114.

[99] Al-Nouri, Qais, Iraqi rural woman's participation in domestic decision – making, Journal of Comparative Family Studies, vol. XXIV, No. 1, 1993, P. 95.

As for marriage, it is not limited to kinship units, i.e., it is an internal marriage (endogamy). As we have mentioned, marriage here is based on the financial offer made, although marriage is not imposed on the gypsy woman, as she is often free to choose a partner, this purely (materialist) tendency exists primarily in the girl. We believe that this is the result of socialization, especially since the gypsy girl begins at an early age to train or work with her parents to practice dancing and singing. From childhood, she began to emulate dancers and singers and imitate them in almost everything.

The researcher noticed this in a concentrated manner among the male and female pupils of Al Islah Primary School in the gypsy village of Fawwar. He investigated this by interviewing students, observing, and surveying the school's teachers. A few cases of Nahawa, cousin's marriage prevention, may occur and the cousin does them as he has a great power and influence over his and his cousin's family while the main purpose of this is to extort money!! In exchange for his silence about this marriage, he takes aa sum of money.

In general, kinship relations are characterized by weakness and begin to decay, as a piece of evidenced for that is the weakness of the commitments that existed among clan members. This is also confirmed by the fact that Al Mukhtar began to take on a greater role than the head of the kinship group or the sheikh of the clan. Also, many members of the gypsy community, especially young people, and juveniles, ignore the name of both of their parents' clans.

The terms of kinship are quite like those used by the people of Iraq, such as special terms like (father, mother, brother, sister, and son) and descriptive kinship terms for distant relatives such as uncle (brother of father) and uncle (brother of mother) ... Etc. These call adjectives are also used for some relatives from wider kinship units or from strangers and these are used politely and respectfully, such as (my uncle, my uncles, etc). The adjectives of call to call a person the (father of someone) (Abu Flan) are used to call him by the name of his eldest son or daughter, and there is no difference between being called after a son or a daughter as the call goes to the eldest one unlike most Iraqi non-gypsy tribes, such as the tribes in the Iraqi oasis of Shathatha. [100]

The system of nicknames is used by Iraqis, for example, the name Ali has a nickname of Abu Hussein or vice versa. And so on with the rest of the names circulating in this regard.

Names are generally influenced by ecology and the economic and social environment. It is also influenced by the current culture of the expanding society (the dominant culture) which is a kind of social adaptation. The names of the elderly are close to and influenced by the Bedouin and rural environment, for example, the names Shukriyah, Fawziya, Allawi, Matar, Khayoun...) The current names of many children are modern and influenced by the city such as (Mustafa, Hazem, Furat, Sahar ...). There are resonant names intended to provoke or draw attention, which are the names of girls, and this is a result of the nature of their professions, among these names are (Bawan, Imtihan, Fatat, Sharbat, Khishfa...).

The clan's name is not accurate for the gypsy groups; it is sometimes used to name kinship units equivalent to the lineage. For most of them,

---

[100] See Aladdin Al Bayyati, Anthropology Between Theory and Practice, Op. Cit.

the term "clan" is used for both the lineage and the clan. We did not find the genealogical trees, or some genealogists and we believe that the following reasons are behind this:

1. The weakness of the ethnocentrism factor of the group due to the nature of their professions generated social ostracism against them (the gypsies), which led some of them to claim to belong to well-known and wide tribes in Iraq and the region such as (Tamim or Shammar).
2. The illiteracy that dominates the gypsy society.
3. Previous permanent travel, instability and mixing with different races.
4. The kinship relationships factor is somewhat weak.

The largest gypsy tribes in Iraq are:

Albo Barood, Albo Swelem, Albo Hleiw, Albo Dikheel, Albo Akar, Albo Murad, Albo Theneiw, Albo Shati, Al Farahda, Al Metairat, Albo Khazam, Albo Nesaif, Al Bodali and Al Newer (the gypsies who are moving among Iraq, Syria, and Jordan) and they are classified as a clan in the gypsy perspective.

The gypsies are not always committed to convergence in housing, but we find that there is a density of a clan or majority of a clan in an area. For instance, in the Fawwar gypsy area, most of its inhabitants are from the Albo Barood clan. Thus, the sheikh of the area (village), Nazim Jabbar, was the sheikh of their clan, although his authority has now been curtailed by the expansion of the Mukhtar's authority. Previously, the sheikh of the area, Bezaiea Taghi, had a voice heard by the gypsies and was the first to be responsible for them in front of the governmental authority and was their representative in its institutions.

In Kamaliya, most of the households gathering there are from the Albo Khazam clan and their sheikh is Ghadban Nimr, assisted by his brother Mohammad, who has a distinctive house in the area (Kamaliya). Its Mukhtars are Arabs living in other neighbourhoods near the neighbourhood of the gypsy's residence.

The data of the fieldwork study showed that the Kamaliya gypsies are distinguished from other gypsy populations as they have a weak commitment to tribal matters, such as consulting the clan concerning private and tribal problems like others. Only 13% of them resorted to the clan for such things, compared to 27% in the rest of the gypsy areas, as in Fawwar being a sample for the other style.

It turns out that these people are more in contact with the clan and that they resort to the clan's sheikh in tribal matters. Generally, these problems are among members of the kinship group (i.e., the gypsies themselves). The difference between the responses of the household heads from the sample in both study samples is that the gypsies living in Kamaliya are in constant contact with the wider community in addition to the constant presence of a police force patrolling the streets of the area, therefore, there was a kind of dispensation with the role of the clan.

The same matter is found in the commitments to the clan, like the commitment to revenge, the payment of blood money, the commitment to the Nahawa (marriage prevention by the cousin), participation in giving opinions and helping poor people of the clan. All of the above are examples of common tribal commitments in Iraq and all over the region's communities that live a Bedouin, rural and sometimes even urban lifestyles.

Generally, the lack of a spirit to help the poor gypsies from the clan is almost highlighted, which indicates the absence of social solidarity. We believe that there are reasons behind that, one of which is the weakness of kinship tendency and the absence of the need for it. Another reason is the weakness of the religious consciousness that supports it, as well as the lack of awareness and familiarity with the tolerant humanitarian message that everyone must hold on which is now advocated by human rights associations and humanitarian organisations. [101]

The fieldwork study shows that the boundaries of the kinship group, to which the heads of families are committed concerning the aspects of revenge, are shrinking in the Kamaliya area more than in other gypsy regions, like Fawwar in particular. In Kamaliya, the highest percentage is restricted to the relatives of the fourth degree, i.e., to cousins. In Fawwar, the highest percentage is (43%) limited to the borders of the clan. As we mentioned, the clan in their perspective is smaller than what we know of its concept, and it sometimes means the gypsy group is available in this area.

Gypsy families do not demand housing near their relatives, as the fieldwork study showed, but vary almost twice higher in Fawwar than in Kamaliya by only (%30.4-13) of the total families of the research sample.

The reasons behind this difference are that the relationships in Fawwar may be relatively stronger, and the difficulty of buying

---

[101] Notice the United Nations Universal Declaration of Human Rights issued on 1-12-1948, Al-Maaref Press, Baghdad.

or renting houses to achieve this condition in Kamaliya led to these results.

The household in the gypsy community:

There is always great confusion between the concepts of the family and the household, and there have been many opinions and points of view from researchers and those interested in this.

Demographers believe that the family is a human unit made up of two or more people who are linked by kinship, marriage, or adoption, and live together having a shared budget. [102]

A family is a group of individuals (whether they are related or not) who live together and share food and other necessities of living or only one person living alone in an independent housing unit. [103]

Anthropologists believe that the family [104] is the social cell that consists of the father, mother, and their children.

It includes all types and forms of family and divides them into a nuclear family (consisting of the parents and their unmarried children), which is also called primary.

---

[102] Ali, Younis Hammadi, Introduction to Demography, University of Mosul, 1985, p. 59.

[103] Ibid., p. 359.

[104] Beals Ralph & Harry, Harry, Introduction to General Anthropology, Vol.1, translated by Mahmoud Al Jawhari, Al Nahdha Press, Cairo, 1965.

The big compound family is divided into two basic patterns: the extended family and the complex family.

The concept of the household refers to what we call the primary, nuclear, or simple family. [105]

As for social scientists, the definition of the family, as stated in the Family Book of Burgess and Locke, is that it is a group of individuals with strong bonds, resulting from the bonds of marriage, blood and adoption, and this group lives in one house and its members – father, mother, and children – are linked by social relationships based on shared interests and goals. [106]

In Arabic, the stem is (Ail) pronounced as (Jaid), and its plural form is (Iyal) pronounced as (Jiyad). The man (ail) which means having a big family as he is a breadwinner, and the woman is (Muaila). [107]

A family is a social unit that depends mainly on the integration of living among the father, mother, and their children, and thus the definition is limited to the nuclear family. Here we adopt the first definition of demographers, while the family in Arabic is mentioned in the dictionary of the Sihah as (the family of the man, i.e., his gobble because he is strengthened by them).

The family are the followers, rather than those who are bound by a descent relationship or a kinship.

---

[105] Al Bayyati, Op. Cit, Pp. 396-397.
[106] Duncan, Mitchell, Dictionary of Sociology, translated by Ihsan al-Hassan, Al-Rashid Press, Baghdad, 1980, pp. 139-140.
[107] Al Razi, Op. Cit, p 466.

This definition also applies to the definition of demographers. We will use the term "family" here because the gypsy community, due to the nature of living, consists of households, because the family includes people who may be relatives, those who became gypsies, their employees or those who are adopted by them.

The nuclear family in its known form is rarely found living alone and in an independent house due to the high cost of living and the nature of their professions that require a group (such as bands, singers, and dancers).

Their work or some of the other works already mentioned, such as (sex work and brokering), need to join hands and the strength of the group to protect themselves against the aggression or excesses of customers.

The household is described as a complex system that has cultural and social potentials required by development processes. [108]

Prof. Dr Qais Al-Nouri believes that this system (household) performs all the social functions in which the main objectives of society are summarized. These functions are. [109]

1. Reproduction function.
2. Preserving the cultural heritage and passing it on to successive generations, through the normalization of individuals and adapting them according to the historically inherited culture of the society.

---

[108] Al-Nouri, Qais, The Family as a Development Project, Cultural Affairs Press, Baghdad, 1994, 5.

[109] Ibid., 5.6.

3. Economic solidarity processes take place in the household with its main productive aspects, as they are nucleus from which the main forms of human living activity emerge.
4. It plays a historical role in the development of various technical means.
5. The household is of central importance in representing the network of social and human ties that it represents as a kinship.
6. Political and legal frameworks that support the unity of society and protect it from the factors of disintegration and decomposition shall be crystallized in the household.
7. The role of the household in ensuring the flow of religious and ritual activities in society.
8. The family has the responsibility to organise the recreational, creative, aesthetic, and artistic aspects of the household's life because it prepares them from early childhood in a way that they benefit from their free time.

The household can therefore be described as a microcosm of the larger society.[110]

So, since this is the role of the household and these are its functions and benefits, its danger equals its benefits if it is invalid or it miseducates and misguides. The family could be the epicentre of delinquency and the base for criminality if it is a deviant family.

---

[110] Ibid., 7.

The household's size:

The term "household's size" simply means the group of individuals who belong to a particular family, and it is not a requirement to be within kinship relationships or lineage, there are factors that affect the size of the family, including fertility, mortality, marriage, gender structure, profession and life cycle of the family and others.

The gypsy household is like the traditional Iraqi household in its large size due in part to polygamy and the shared residence of married children.

Table -2- Iterative distribution of the number of members of the sample households in the two study areas.

Area	Kamaliya	Fawwar
Category	Iteration	Iteration
6-4	14	11
9-7	12	18
12-10	12	10
15-13	11	5
18-16	2	2
21-19	3	-
Total	54	46

It is clear from the data in the table above that the disparity between the study areas in the size of the household is not large. The amount of the arithmetic mean of the Kamaliya area was (10.2) individuals out of number of studied household members in the area with a standard deviation of (4.2).

As for the Fawwar area, arithmetic mean of the number of the studied household members was (9) individuals with a standard deviation of (3).

This means that the size of the gypsy household, in general, is high and very large compared to the size of the households in the world particularly in the Kamaliya area. It appears that the reasons behind the rise in the size of the gypsy household in the Kamaliya area are the following:

1. It is an attraction for gypsies, due to the availability of job opportunities because of its location near the capital Baghdad as (nightclubs, restaurants, clubs and halls that organise parties) are available in Baghdad. The openness of Baghdadi's society has also created more job opportunities for them. Thus, many of the Kamaliya gypsies' relatives or workers of them came to Kamaliya and lived in shared residences with families of Kamaliya gypsies.

2. The rise in housing property prices in Baghdad makes it difficult to buy new houses. The sudden rise in the prices of construction materials was due to the conditions of the siege on Iraq also makes it difficult to buy new houses and thus causing difficulty of familial fission.

3. There is also a restriction by neighbouring Arabs (non-gypsy) on the expansion of the role of the gypsies in the area. There was a decision by the government that prevented unregistered people in the 1977 census and earlier in Baghdad from owning property in Baghdad. [111]

---

[111] Bariyat: Plural and singular word, which refers to a mat woven from reed slices after cutting or hammering it longitudinally and it is made in the marshlands of southern Iraq.

Concerning the nature of the structure of the gypsy household (as heads of households, wives, children and relatives) according to the fieldwork study sample, it is clear to us that the total number of males in the Kamaliya area reached (271) to represent (53%) of the total number of members of the studied group of the study sample in Kamaliya area and the total number of females reached (237) to represent (47%).

As for Fawwar area, the number of males was (197) representing (50.4%) compared to (194) females representing (49.6%). The total number of children was (320) representing (63%) of the total sample members in Kamaliya. In the Fawwar area, the total number of children was (270) to be (69%) of the total study sample in the area.

The total number of relatives residing with the households of their relatives in the Kamaliya area was (112) divided into (62 males) and (50 from Alana), and (22%) of the total study sample in the Kamaliya area. In comparison, the number of relatives in the Fawwar area (50 people) was divided into (28 females) and (22 males) representing (13%) of the total members of the study sample in the area.

It is clear from all this that:
1. The percentage of gender (male to female) in the two study areas is almost equal to the percentage of gender in Iraqi society.
2. The percentage of relatives who are with the households of their relatives is very high or is more in Kamaliya than in Fawwar, which is due to several reasons, among them:

Most of these relatives are residents for work because of the availability of job opportunities in the Kamaliya area due to its location and the high prices of housing rents and for housing decline in the gypsies in Kamaliya. Some of these relatives are in-laws and reside with their wives' families, which is called in Iraq (Qa'idi marriage), and we found an example of this (three in-laws) residing in the house of their wives' families. It is also worth mentioning that some of what they call relatives already became gypsies.

There are also some people looking for work in the gypsy areas or expatriates from the reality of their lives who preferred to live in the gypsy areas or some of those who were adopted by the gypsies as children.

Women are heads of household in the gypsy community:

According to the fieldwork study, it was found that a considerable number of heads of household were females and in the two study areas. Their number in Kamaliya was (13 women) representing (24%) of the total sample. In Fawwar area, the number of women as heads of household was (11 women) and the Kamaliya area shared the same percentage.

This is the result of the multiple divorces resulting from marriage failures and from the importance of women's role as a source of income and support for the family.

The age group (30-34) was more in terms of the belonging of heads of households to the gypsies. The reason behind that was that they represented the beginning of independence for families and the beginning of family fission.

Table 3 - The marital status of the head of the household and his relationship with it (the household).

Kamaliya

Marital status	Father	Mother	Brother	Sister	Total	%
Adjective						
Married*	22	-	6	-	28	52
Single	-	-	6	2	8	15
Divorced	2	6	1	2	11	20
Widower	4	2	-	1	7	13
Total	28	8	13	5	45	100
%	52	15	24	9	100	100

Fawwar

Marital status	Father	Mother	Brother	Sister	Total	%
Adjective						
Married*	20	-	5	-	25	54
Single	-	-	5	1	6	13
Divorced	2	6	-	1	9	20
Widower	3	2	-	1	6	13
Total	25	8	10	3	46	100
%	54	17	22	7	100	100

*Means currently married (at the time of the study)

Marital status:

From the data in the table above, the rates appear to be similar in the two study areas, and the following appeared:

1. Most of the heads of households are fathers and this goes along with the authority of the father, i.e., it is a patriarchal society.

2. Brothers come second as the heads of households; they are generally the older brothers in the household. As a result of the loss of the father due to death or his long absence, the older brother is responsible for the household, and that is also an expression of parental authority and a kind of social solidarity and cohesion.

3. If there is no older brother who can ensure the living or the management of the household, the mother is responsible for and the head of the household, which is an affirmation of the role of the woman and the mother.

4. What also confirms the role and status of the woman is to be responsible for or the breadwinner of her family or for a large household. That is undoubtedly the result of their economic role as a productive individual with a dependent economic income primarily in the gypsy society.

5. A relatively high percentage of divorced and widowed heads of households, especially women (mother and sister), appeared because most of the marriages made to them were for material purposes. Some gypsy girls are married to non-gypsy people in exchange for a large material deal. This marriage ends shortly after satisfying the whim and libido of this person so that this girl returns to her parents divorced even if she has one or more children, as these marriages were not based on a family stay.

Table -4- Number of marriages of the household's heads

Kamaliya

Number of times	Males	Females	Total	%
1	18	5	23	50
2	10	3	13	28
3	3	2	5	11
4	3	1	4	9
5	-	-	-	-
More than 5	1		1	2
Total	35	11	46	100

Fawwar

Number of times	Males	Females	Total	%
1	14	4	18	45
2	9	3	12	30
3	4	2	6	15
4	2	1	3	7.5
5	1	-	1	2.5
More than 5	-	-	-	-
Total	30	10	40	100

Through the data of this table, the number of times of marriages of about half of the research sample of married households' heads was limited to one time. This means that the rest of the percentage exceeded one to two times or more. This percentage is high and there is no doubt that it indicates several things, among which are:

1. Encouraging polygamy, some of which may be illegal and not last long, and we found one of the old household's heads in Kamaliya who got married seven times in his lifetime for economic purposes.
2. The large number of divorces due to failed marriages, which we pointed out earlier.
3. The convergence of the two areas of study in this aspect indicates the unity of thinking of the gypsies in this aspect and the relative similarity of their circumstances.

Data show that there is polygamy, and the fieldwork study showed that as some gypsies had more than one wife in one or more houses if their financial condition was good enough for it. Having multiple wives is allowed by Islamic law for no more than four wives to have at once. However, the economic circumstances resulting from the economic blockade, polygamy.

Table -5- Age at the time of the first marriage.

Area	Kamaliya				Fawwar			
Age/ gender	Males	Female	Total	%	Males	Female	Total	%
Under 15 yrs.	1	2	3	6.5	-	2	2	5
15-19	3	5	8	18	4	4	8	20
20-24	19	4	23	50	17	4	21	52.5
25-29	10	-	10	22	8	-	8	20
30 and more	2	-	2	4.5	1	-	1	2.5
Total	35	11	46	100	30	10	10	100

From the table above, the data shows that the highest percentage of the households' heads ages when they got married for the first time stops at the age range of (20-25) years for males in both of the study areas. For women, the age range (15-19) years comes in first place, followed by the age range of (24-29) in the second place for men, and the age range of (20-24) years for women.

It is also noted through the data that some female heads of households from the sample got married at an early age of 15 and this marriage is always done for dowries and even (large financial transactions).

The educational status of the gypsies:

The educational level of the household heads is of great importance in the upbringing and guidance of children and household management. That is a scale for the living and economic level, and the educated person has good adaptability as well.

The study data showed the following:
1. The illiteracy rate is generally high among gypsy household heads.
2. The illiteracy rate in the Kamaliya area is lower than it in Fawwar area as an example of other gypsy areas in Iraq as far as the households' heads are concerned. That was so because of the prolonged stability of the gypsies in the first area, which means that the opportunity for education is possible, even if it was a small one. The opportunity for education has also been enriched by improved living conditions, and the availability of services as Kamaliya was approximately near Baghdad.
3. The highest level of education of the heads of gypsy households is a primary school, which consists (of 5 persons) a male and a woman in Kamaliya two of them in Fawwar.

It can be judged that most gypsies are unproductive consumers according to data that indicated that a total of (201) children are under the age of (15 years). This means that they are under the age of legal work or self-reliance, which means that they depend on their families. But, away from the numbers, we say that if this applies to males, we exclude females because they represent the economic base on which the gypsy economy is based, where girls of young ages starting from the age of (10 years) are involved in dance performances. As for the age (14 or 15 years), it is the age of maturity and the peak of giving for the gypsy girl. Sometimes she is married off by her parents for a very high price, usually to non-gypsy man. These marriages are a total failure and then the girl returns (to satisfy all customers' wishes).

Most boys and even those of working age are dependent on their households and rely mainly on girls for the cost of living.

Table – 6 – Classifying children according to gender and age category in Fawwar

Gender	Sons		Daughters		Total	
Age category	Number	%	Number	%	Number	%
0-5	39	28	35	27	74	27
6-10	32	23	25	19.2	57	21.1
11-15	27	19	17	13.1	44	16.3
16-20	16	11.3	20	15.4	36	13.3
21-25	10	7	17	13.1	27	10
26-30	7	5	9	7	16	6
31-35	5	4	4	3.1	9	3.3
36-40	3	2	1	0.7	4	1.5
40-	1	0.7	2	1.3	3	1.1
Total	140	100	130	100	270	100

categories of the gypsy household in Fawwar with its counterpart in Kamaliya. We would like to point out that some girls are over thirty years old, i.e. older than the normal age of marriage for several reasons among which are:

1. Either she is married and with her husband in her parents' house, i.e. (Qa'idi marriage).
2. Or she is divorced because most marriages fail as we indicated earlier.
3. Or her marriage is delayed by her will or acquiescence to the will of her household to make her work for the household.

The Qualitative composition of relatives:

Table – 7 – Classifying relatives according to gender and age category in Kamaliya.

Gender	Male relatives		Female relatives		Total	
Age category	Number	%	Number	%	Number	%
0-5	4	6.5	3	6	7	6.3
6-10	4	6.5	5	10	9	8
11-15	6	9.7	5	10	11	10
16-20	8	13	7	14	15	13.4
21-25	15	24.2	13	26	28	25
26-30	12	19.3	12	24	24	21.4
31-35	7	11.3	2	4	9	8
36-40	2	3.2	1	2	3	2.7
41-45	1	1.6	1	2	2	1.7
46-50	2	3.2	1	2	3	2.7
51-55	1	1.6			1	0.8
56-60						
61-65						
66-70						
71-						
Total	62	100	50	100	112	100

In the above table, it is noted that the age category (21-25 years) ranked first among the relatives' age categories, and their members were (28 individuals) of both genders representing (25%), followed by the age category (26-30 years) representing (21.4%) and then comes the category (16-20 years) representing (13.4 %).

These categories are the peak of activity, work and giving in the gypsy community and the world as well, and it became obvious to us that most of these relatives reside here in Kamaliya for the purpose of work as opportunities are more available here, and some of those gypsies migrated from other gypsy areas in the provinces.

Table – 8 - Classifying relatives according to gender and age category in Fawwar.

Gender	Male relatives		Female relatives		Total	
Age category	Number	%	Number	%	Number	%
0-5	2	9	2	7	4	8
6-10	2	9	1	4	3	6
11-15	1	5	1	4	2	4
16-20	2	9	4	14.2	6	12
21-25	4	18	8	28.6	12	24
26-30	4	18	7	25	11	12
31-35	3	13	2	7	5	10
36-40	1	5	1	4	2	4
41-45	2	9	1	4	3	6
46-50	-	-	-	-	-	-
51-55	-	-	1	4	1	2
56-60	1	5			1	2
61-65						
66-70						
71-						
Total	22	100	28	100	50	100

In the table above, we find out that most of the relatives residing with gypsy households in Fawwar gypsy area are in the age category of (21-25 years) and they were (12 people) divided into (4 males) and (8 females) representing (24%) followed by the category (26-30 years) representing (22%) and then came the category (16-20 years).

These categories represent the young age phase and the active economic power of the gypsies because their professions depend on the age of young people, especially girls.

It was also obvious that the number of woman relatives is more than the number of males in the area, as there were (28 individuals) of them representing (56%) of the number of relatives residing with gypsy households in the area.

It is noted that the proportion of relative female in Fawwar is higher than in the Kamaliya area. As I pointed out, most of these relatives became gypsies and especially women, most of them are pleasure vendors (sex workers) who have abandoned their homes and areas and sought refuge in gypsy areas for various reasons. The difference between the two areas in terms of the increase in women's number who were considered relatives of households is that the gypsy girls would prefer gypsy areas other than Kamaliya because they are isolated and far from the eyes of the police and the cities.

The educational level of children and relatives:

Gypsy society is generally characterized by alphabetical and cultural illiteracy, although the law of Compulsory Education and Literacy in Iraq has been applied to them since 1978 until now. The reason behind illiteracy and ignorance is due to the following:

1. The instability of the gypsies until recently, as households continue to move from one gypsy area to the other either for subjective reasons or for reasons which are beyond their control such as the deliberate displacement imposed on them by the government. That what was happened to their places of settlement in (Abu Sha'ir in Musayyib in Babylon Province, Al Sharaka Al Gharbiya in Muthanna, Al-Sahaji in Mosul, Al Othmaniya Al Amiriyah and Al Fajr in Dhi Qar Province, Abu Ghraib and Al-Tarab neighbourhood in Al Zubair in Basra Province).

2. Schools are far from their places of settlement.

3. Social ostracism, and the scorn that their children face from their classmates and teachers in the schools they join.

4. Poor motivation for education due to their dispensation with reading and writing because most of their professions do not require them. They also excluded the idea of working in a government profession or working for non-gypsies.

5. Households' poor family awareness in general and their improper socialization and guidance of children and not urging them to continue their education. The household also usually falls short of the rights of its pupils, and we found out how severely negligent the pupils' parents of Al Islah Primary School in the gypsy village of Fawwar were. Most pupils are in a deplorable condition as some people's clothes are shabby, some look bad, and others have no care for hygiene. They lack the motivation to be self and group esteemed, and they feel inferior to non-gypsies even though some of them have the motivation to educate, look into the future and integrate into wider society.

Most gypsy children evade school especially at the primary level, in most gypsy areas in Iraq. That is not the case for the Kamaliya area as there is some motivation there more than in other areas due to its location in Baghdad, the capital, and the constant civilized contact and interaction. Those factors resulted in greater adaptation than other gypsy areas. In Fawwar area, we did not find anyone with an intermediate school degree as the highest level of education was either to fail or drop out of school in the third intermediate or lower.

In the Kamaliya area, it is somehow different, as some gypsies passed this grade, but very few of them.

Conclusion

1. The size of the gypsy household in Kamaliya area appeared to be up to (10.2 members) while the size of its counterpart in Fawwar area was (9 members). We mentioned earlier that this size and disparity is due to: the difficulty of family fission because of the high cost of living in general, the high cost of house buying and renting in Kamaliya, and that the nature of their professions needs strength and numerical abundance to face the customers' aggressions and assaults, as well as shared residence accommodation with their relatives' households. The last reason is the numbers of people who became gypsies (sex workers and gypsy workers).
2. The gypsy household is complex and has a shared residence.
3. The alphabetical and cultural illiteracy[112] prevails in the gypsy

---

[112] Cultural illiteracy refers to general ignorance of science, literature, technology, and the broad context of life (etiquette) or the so-called etiquette of cohabitation.

community despite the availability of (primary) schools near their communities, and the highest levels of education reached by the gypsies are to pass the primary level for many of them. The study did not show that anyone had passed the intermediate grade.

4. The gypsy area in Kamaliya is more fortunate in terms of the availability of educational opportunities as schools at all levels and types (preparatory, vocational, etc.) are very close. Schools here are also coeducational for gypsies and Arabs (non-gypsies) in the area offering the opportunity to acquire cultural traits and interaction and thus to adapt to some extent to the prevailing culture.

The marriage system in the gypsy community:

Marriage is the sacred bond according to which two people (traditionally a man and a woman) are connected in order to satisfy several desires, perhaps the most important of which are (sexual instinct, having children, starting a family that provides them with a better life). And then their responsibilities extend further to satisfy the desire of human society to preserve and continue the human species and reassure its psychological and social needs.

Marriage is a social system that includes a few less complex systems, each of which, however, includes many interrelated elements and phenomena, such as the dowry system and the network of social relations between the two kinship groups to which the spouses belong. [113]

---

[113] Ismail, Farouk, Cultural Anthropology, University Knowledge House, Alexandria, 1989, pp. 133-134.

Gypsy society, like other human societies, has this human instinct. As for its controls and systems, they are the same as in other Islamic societies, because of their adherence to Islam, and Iraqi customs and traditions are used to apply this. This is the result of continuous civilized contact and coexistence with those traditions and customs. As a manifestation of that contact, the gypsies always conduct wedding parties in their neighboring areas and throughout Iraq in the countryside and the city. There is no doubt that they were greatly influenced by society's ceremonies, traditions and ways of marriage.

Like the Islamic societies, three forms of marriage dominate the gypsy community:

1. Monogamy: it is a one-time marriage of a man. It is now prevalent due to the high dowry and the difficult cost of living, and urban communication has a big role as it has influenced the urban life that has become its character as well...

2. Polygamy: it does not exceed four wives who are alive and bound to him by a religious and official bond, at the same time, according to Islamic law. This was prevalent until recently before the settlement of the gypsies, and now it has receded into a narrow range for the reasons mentioned above.

3. Levitate marriage: it is when the brother marries his brother's widow, or the sister marries her sister's widower. This kind of marriage is common in patriarchal societies.

Such a type has many functions and benefits, including:

a. Taking care of the children with their uncle.

b. Preserving the wealth of the deceased brother, by not transferring it with the widow or children to the new husband.

c. Strengthens kinship and builds bridges again with the wife, her family and the children of the deceased.

Marriage in the gypsy community is not limited to the boundaries of a kinship group or unit, such as cousins, for example, or even a tribe, which means that it is not endogamy, rather it is exogamy, especially to non-gypsies. The purpose behind the exogamy is purely financial, as this (stranger) pays a very high dowry, and some gypsy dowries reached (one hundred and fifty thousand dinars-about 25 thousand dollars). These marriages were purely material deals and were done with the consent of the girl. These marriages were either illegal or illegitimate and end with the girl's return to her parents after a short period of time when the primary purpose of marriage had been reached, which is the fulfillment of the temporal love, attraction, sexual desires and temptation. The girl is always required to be a virgin in such marriages (see the chapter on social adaptation – affinity).

Although exogamy does not support kinship and weakens it, according to their point of views, earning money is the most important aspect, and this aspect is most applicable to the concept of social exchange, which the scientist Peter Blau interprets as: "optional voluntary actions of individuals motivated by the benefits expected or actually achieved from others"[114].

The age of marriage among the gypsies is delayed for males, especially for females (except for marriage deals with strangers, which are unsuccessful and temporary). Generally, they are done at an early age.

---

[114] Zeitlin, contemporary social theory, already mentioned, P.148.

Table -9- obstacles that delay the age of marriage.

Obstacles / area	Dowry rise	Working for the household	Other	Total
Kamaliya	36	15	3	54
%	66.6	28	5.4	100
Fawwar	30	12	4	46
%	65	26	9	100

It is clear from the data of the above table that the rise of dowries is the main reason for the late marriage age, as the percentage reached (66.6%) in Kamaliya, and (65%) in Fawwar, where dowries reached very high numbers compared to dowries in the rest of Iraq.

The reason behind the rise in dowries here is that women are a very important source of economic income, and it is not easy to dispense this source without getting compensation for it.

This is because (28 %) of the gypsy women work for the benefit of the household in Kamaliya and (26 %) of them do the same thing in Fawwar, and the percentage here is close in both regions, which confirms (the unity of the gypsies).

The other reasons that were not indicated are (sexual desire satisfaction in the region, high costs of living in general, instability and others), these came in third place.

Most of the study samples believe that the ideal age for marriage is (21-25) years old, which is the same for girls and in both study areas.

After the fieldwork study and the use of interview forms, we were informed that there is great freedom for both the young man and the young woman to choose their life partner and that the issue of coercion in marriage is almost absent in the gypsy community.

We must draw attention to the fact that some gypsies may exaggerate or lie in their answers to go along with what is prevailing in society to avoid the embarrassment that they encounter with non-gypsies.

The gypsies' marriage ceremonies:

The engagement, wedding and marriage ceremonies are no different from those in Iraqi society, especially in the areas adjacent to the gypsy communities.

Men and women have a wide freedom to be together. When someone like a girl, he tells his family about her, or he consults his family to choose a girl for marriage.

The young man's mother goes with his sister or one of the women of the area or relatives to the house of the chosen girl. The conversation is held between the mothers first and then the girl's opinion is taken and if she gives the green light, the man's mother returns and tells his father, older brother or guardian and goes with a group of notables of the region to the girl's family house. When she offers them coffee or tea, they do not drink until they get a pledge to fulfil their request and the purpose for which they came. After giving them that, they drink and talk about the topic of engagement. The consent is finally taken when the girl agrees.

The dowry and the marriage supplies are determined, which is called (the wedding requirements), and as we mentioned, the dowry is very high, especially for a very beautiful girl. After the wedding date is set, preparations are made days before the wedding date then the party is held, which is usually on Thursday (i.e. Friday night), which is a blessed day in the belief of Muslims. The night before the wedding day is called (henna night) in which the betrotheds' hands are decorated with henna separately each in his/her family's house with the presence of his/her family and friends and a big party is held in the groom's house, and a similar one for women in the bride's house.

On the wedding day, food is usually prepared (sacrifices of sheep and calves, rice and broth are cooked, spirits are prepared, a tent is usually set up to receive male guests, and the party is held at night and in the presence of both men and women. The wedding is considered when the groom and the bride ride in a car side by side and followed by the cars of friends, family and relatives with a large procession accompanied by a folk music band playing along the way where they go to the nearest shrine. In Fawwar, the wedding cars often go out to Diwaniyah because of its closeness, and the wedding cars roam near the shrine of Imam Abul-Fadl. Then they roam in some of the streets of Diwaniyah before getting back to the gypsy area. Men start shooting in the air to celebrate the occasion, when the wedding cars go out of the city to avoid police as shooting is illegal.

The marriage bond is registered in court in advance, of course, and another religious contract is performed by (Al Sayyed) or (cleric), who is a man of religion, and is usually a non-gypsy.

After dinner, the groom is introduced to his bride by one of the dignitaries who leads him to the door. The groom changes his clothes inside the room after greeting his wife. The party is held and continues until late at night, from this a common proverb was derived (a wedding of Al Kawliya) which implies that work should be given to its specialists, or it implies exaggerating in doing something.

The husband's entry into his wife for the first time is accompanied by zaghrats and chants such as: (bless your wedding, you the notable), (a groom and his friends celebrating him), (the best of luck and you deserve her).

After the husband enters his wife, he greets her and kisses her forehead. The husband's mother washes the groom's and bride's legs together in one bowl and puts the groom's leg on top of his bride's bag so that he is the master and the one obeyed in the house, as he thought so.

Conclusion

A conclusion can be reached, which is embodied in the following points:
1. The descent in the gypsy society is patrilineal, inheritance and succession are in the male line.
2. The combined and common family is the dominant model in the gypsy community.
3. The gypsy women have a high status in the gypsy household and society because they are a source of income, and this confirms the hypothesis that "the position of an individual in the household depends on his/her economic role". Another indication of this is

the preference for having girls over boys. This applies to the status of close relatives in the household, since their status depends on the extent of their economic role in the household. We explained this based on the propositions of the exchange theory.

4. Kinship relations are weak within the broader kinship units, and their strength is almost Limited within the family.

5. The terms of kinship and marriage models are like those that exist in the prevailing culture (Iraqi society).

6. The marriage age is delayed among kinship groups.

7. Images of social adaptation appear in many aspects of kinship systems, including (exogamy, the use of kinship and epithets that exist in the Iraqi society "the prevailing culture", title and name system) as well as the system of marriage and its ceremonies.

8. The correspondence between the two study areas appears in most aspects of this chapter, except that kinship relations are relatively wider and stronger in Fawwar area than them in Kamaliya area.

Chapter Five

Religious Pattern

The concept of religion

The gypsies' Religious Practices

Conclusion of the chapter

The concept of religion

Religion in the Arabic language: A general name given to everything through which God is worshipped, as well as several meanings, including king, sultan, oppression, obedience, judiciary, custom, doctrine and sharia.

In the Islamists' terminology, it is:

"Religion sets the divine driver for those with minds by choosing Him to be righteous in status and financially successful. According to Durkheim's definition: religion is a mutually reinforcing set of beliefs and actions concerning sacred things, beliefs and deeds that unite their followers in a moral unit called the Milla". [115]

From the definitions of religion above despite their variations, whether linguistic or idiomatic, Islamic, or non-Islamic, we observe that they agree on the pattern that regulates or shows the shape of the relationship between the Creator and the creature or what the creature perceives or assumes as being its Creator. Therefore, it shows the obligations it performs towards Him. The religious pattern studies the form of these beliefs, their impact on human societies, the strength of their influence on the path of life of these societies and the extent of their power to influence and control the lives of individuals in respecting and adhering to these beliefs.

---

[115] Alyan, Rushdi and Samouk, Saadoun, Religions: A Comparative Historical Study, Ministry of Higher Education Press, Baghdad, 1976, pp. 19-23.

Durkheim also sees religion as "a system of beliefs and practices connected to sacred things". [116]

In his view, this means that we can recognize religion through what a people believe and think in this aspect or what is applied to the sacred ideas they hold, and that is religion reflecting its beliefs and practices on society.

From this, it can be understood that there are no people, no matter how advanced they may be in civilization, who have no religion. But the difference among nations and peoples in this regard lies in the varying degrees to which their religions are developed. The simplest of these are the primitive ones, which are embodied in the form of simple and naïve beliefs resulting from hypotheses made by those primitive people mixed with different magical practices and rituals. [117] That represents the mentality of those people. Some religions express the ideas of people with advanced minds which are considered wise and reformers that put their conceptions about the universe and creation and drew up regulations to guide humankind in the absence of divine religions such as Buddha, Confucius, [118] Zoroaster and others. The monotheistic religions are the finest in terms of their degree of persuasion and modernity, and they are adopted by the most advanced civilized societies.

Religion is embodied in a behavioural and moral legal system, and the relationship between the worshipper and the idol takes the form of

---

116 Mair, Lucy, Introduction to Social Anthropology, translated by Shakir Salim, Al Hurriah Press, Baghdad, 1983, p. 256.
117 See Lucy Mair, Introduction to Social Anthropology, chapters 13 and 14.
118 See Alian and Samuk, Op. Cit.

a prescribed fixed social pattern. The most important features of the religious faith are holding emotional attitudes towards the idol and behaving in a specific method of approaching him and conducting celebrations and rituals.[119]

Religion has definitions with many points of view that vary according to the sciences that deal with it, as it relates to it. The religious structure of the population is of great importance because it often expresses national loyalty by certain groups. Religious and sectarian differences also play an important role in shaping decisions regarding many aspects of human life.

United Nations experts recommended the inclusion of religion in population censuses of 1970-1980 as one of the geographically and socially beneficial topics. [120]

Gypsies' Religious Practices:

The prevailing belief among most members of Iraqi society is that gypsies have no religion. They are also ignorant of many of the ritual practices and ceremonies carried out by the gypsies that are related to many matters of life such as marriage, circumcision, ceremonies to prepare the dead to be buried and other methods of vital transactions, whether in terms of worship or transactions.

---

[119] Lucy Mair, Introduction to Social Anthropology, Op. Cit, p. 461.
[120] Hamadi Ali, Younis, Op. Cit, p. 394.

We say here that the most important of what is understood about the gypsies in most parts of the world is that they colour (like a chameleon), and in the most important contexts of life, including religion, language, and fashion according to the environment in which they reside. Therefore, that is considered as a kind of social compatibility and adaptation, especially in material aspects.

Thus, the gypsies here in Iraq are religious to Islam if Islam is the official state religion and the religion of the society in which they live.

The perception that others hold here about the gypsies is the result of the gypsies' doing jobs that are contrary to the teachings of the Islamic religion. Furthermore, the deeds of some of them are regarded as contrary to the law and the values of society besides the wrong rumoured ideas about some of them in the eyes of non-gypsies.

The gypsy here lives in great duality, he answers you when you ask him about his religion that he is a Muslim and that he is aware of the limits of God and his religion. On the other hand, you can note that he does not apply the simplest rules of the Islamic religion and that the professions and jobs that most of them are committed to are completely contrary to the Islamic religion.

In some of the studied sample members' houses, we found the Qur'an, the Islamic holy book, but at the same time, there is a place for sex work in this house, a shop for selling alcoholic beverages attached to the house, and places for parties of dancing and singing.

Most gypsies also frequently visit religious shrines near their gatherings, and some of them are committed to religious occasions, but they soon return to the way they were.

In most aspects of their ritual lives, the gypsies are committed to the rules of the Islamic religion, some of which are applied as official laws in the state to ease transactions.

For example, marriage is carried out similarly as it is in the rest of the Muslim community by following a legal formula, and the marriage contract is ratified in court, preceded, or followed by a religious contract by a cleric called the Al Sayyed, Mullah or (Momen).

This Sayyed is usually from outside the gypsy community and until recently there was no one in any gypsy area to carry out this work, because of their ignorance of religious matters. However, we found that some gypsies appeared to perform this task professionally or semi-professionally.

Regarding polygamy, the gypsy individual is committed, in this respect, to the teachings of the Islamic religion, as no more than four wives may be combined at the same time. There is no doubt that this commitment is the result of multiple factors among which is that this religious rule became a legal provision.

We believe that there are other things that bind that. Among these are the economic reasons, such as high dowries, the high cost of living, as well as the inability to combine more than one wife due to many problems that occur as a result, not to mention the possibility of satisfying the libido in the atmosphere available in the area.

One of the commitments that the gypsies have because of their conversion to Islam is the process of circumcision of boys, which takes place at an early age, which is an important obligation in the Islamic religion.

As for the religious ceremonies of preparing and praying on the dead and the burial procedures, which are done according to the teachings of the Islamic religion, the gypsies are completely ignorant of them, because of their ignorance of the teachings of the religion. In this case, the gypsy individual pre-prepares the funeral and then takes it to the burial place which is usually located nearby or in the same area where the dead body is washed, it is called (Al Mughaisil). In general, as a kind of social adaptation that we referred to, the gypsies of the southern area, including Fawwar, bury their dead in the Najaf cemetery, and Kamaliya gypsies do the same thing influenced by the communities surrounding them (the rest of Kamaliya's non-gypsy population) influenced them.

After the burial, ceremonies are held in the house of the deceased's family to accept condolences, it is called Al Fatiha. They continue for three days, and the mourners visit the deceased's family to read Al Fatiha. Of course, most of those interested in these ceremonies know how to read Surah al-Fatiha because they need it.

In-kind gifts such as some bags of food items such as rice, sugar or others are offered. However, this habit decreased and even faded in the difficult conditions of the siege, but, generally, amounts of money, called (wajib), are offered by the mourners according to their financial ability. Nowadays, the amount of money ranges between (25-100 dinars about half a dollar to two dollars) on average. This is a kind of expression of social solidarity among the members of the gypsy community. Household members of the deceased and some of his relatives wear black as an expression of grief and a kind of loyalty to the deceased.

The fieldwork study of the Kamaliya and Fawwar areas showed that all samples of the study are Muslim gypsies (knowing that all Iraqi gypsies are Muslims) and that every one of them knows their affiliation.

But when we asked the following question: (What is your religion?) to 18 (eighteen) pupils of both genders, in the primary school of the Fawwar gypsy area, he found out that the answer to his question was silence, as no one of them knows his/her religion. Perhaps they understood the question wrongly or did not hear it, so the teacher of Islamic education repeated the question to them.!! He was also surprised by someone's answer that his religion was Christianity.!! That was the answer although they were familiar with the name of the Prophet Muhammad and some of his companions, and that the Creator is God Almighty.

There is no doubt that these children lack their families' guidance and religious upbringing. What they learn from school is a lesson like the rest of the lessons and is just an indoctrination that they can memorize and forget quickly.

The fieldwork study also showed that some gypsy families keep the Holy Quran at their homes, and we found that only five people in Kamaliya and seven in Fawwar claimed to have a copy of the Qur'an. This means that there is a low percentage of those who keep the Holy Qur'an. This is due to several reasons, the most important of which is: the gypsies' lack of religious commitment and their alphabetical and religious illiteracy, as well as the incompatibility of the behaviour of some of them with the principles of the Islamic religion.

It appears that this percentage is higher in Fawwar than in Kamaliya, and we see that the reasons relate to the frequent visits of the people of Fawwar area to the nearby holy areas (Najaf and Karbala). They also continue to connect to a conservative and less open society, unlike the situation in Kamaliya. This does not mean that everyone who kept the Qur'an at their home read it, but it can be a mostly superficial commitment. It appears that the number of people who read the Qur'an in Kamaliya is more than in Fawwar, and this is because the percentage of people who know how to read and write in the first area is more than that in the second one.

The few numbers of people who read the Qur'an is the same number of those who listen to the Qur'an as well, whether by listening to it through a person, television, radio or recorder, and a different place, whether at home, mosque, car or shop.

We found that very few gypsies who commit to the duties of prayer and fasting in the study areas (Kamaliya and Fawwar).

Table – 10 – The numbers and percentage of those who pray within the study area.

Area	Yes	%	No	%	Total
Kamaliya	3	6	51	94	54
Fawwar	10	22	36	78	46
Total	13	13	87	87	100

Table – 11- The numbers and percentage of those who fast Ramadhan within the study sample.

Area	Yes	%	No	%	Total
Kamaliya	3	6	51	94	54
Fawwar	10	22	36	78	46
Total	13	13	87	87	100

The percentage of those who pray in Fawwar area appears to be more than that in the Kamaliya area. The same thing applies to those who fast during Ramadan and those who do not. As mentioned before, the explanation for that is that this area (Fawwar) lies close to a relatively conservative community and the holy places, unlike the Kamaliya area, as it lies in a more open area, which is the capital, Baghdad.

This was reflected in both regions. As a result of this reflection, the gypsies of the Fawwar area are distinguished from their counterparts in Kamaliya in that they have one mosque and three Husseiniyas. These mosques may come form of a reception room (diwaniya), or mudhif, and its door is open towards the outside of the house. People from the area prepared them and attached them to their homes or they opened the door of the reception room towards the outside of the house to become a mosque.

These places do not witness any form of worship, they are dedicated to hospitality, drinking tea and coffee, and discussing matters related to the region by its people. We noticed and listened to what was going on in these places throughout the fieldwork study and coexistence in the region.

As a kind of social adaptation to their neighbouring environment, gypsies can be seen frequently visiting holy shrines, especially Karbala and Najaf, in line with what the people of the neighbouring community do. They perform similar rituals to what the people of neighbouring regions do during the visit, such as modesty and reverence, and they pretend to adhere to that, especially in the month of Muharram its tenth day (Ashura), which is the day of (the martyrdom of Imam Hussein bin Ali). That goes in line with what Shiite Muslims do in terms of grief and work suspension on this day, as they suspend their work and some of them grant reward (such as food and tea).

We can see that these acts work suspension, and such are a kind of social adaptation in the first place as mentioned earlier. Their activities do not exist currently, not because they do not want to, but rather it is a result of the fact that those who visit them frequently stop doing that during these days and on the Day of Ashura in particular. This happens especially in the Fawwar area, where most of the people of the neighbouring areas are Shiites, or as a kind of atonement ritual.

For Kamaliya gypsies, these manifestations are less severe than in Fawwar, because they are in Baghdad, which includes a mixture of religions and sects. However, the reason for the (relative) adherence of the Kamaliya gypsies is that the rest of the residents of the Kamaliya and the neighbouring areas are of the Shiite sect. Their adherence is also due to adaptation reasons and to avoid the possibility of fanaticism and the revenge of some of the people neighbouring the gypsies against them, because of their direct contact with them.

Gypsies believe a lot in metaphysical matters and magic. We noticed a lot of manifestations that indicate this, including what is believed to bring luck, such as (beads), (what guards against envy) such as supplication and amulets, like (what captures the hearts of others) of the opposite sex, as it is believed, such as (buzzband) which is the bone of a hoopoe or hedgehog or something else. That is read on by a magician and own it in his name. That also includes (what brings luck and reassurance) such as supplications and Quranic verses in addition to (Alaq), which is a small strip of cloth that they bring for a price or for free from holy shrines.

Table – 12 – Percentage of those who believe in magic through amulets.

Area	Yes	%	No	%	Total
Kamaliya	25	46	29	54	54
Fawwar	30	65	16	35	46
Total	55	55	45	45	100

The high percentage of faith in these matters appears because of religious ignorance and illiteracy. As for the Kamaliya area, the percentage decreases in comparison to Fawwar area because of the cultural contact with Baghdad.

Table – 13 – Percentage of those who carry amulets and their kinds.

Area	Kamaliya		Fawwar	
Type	Repetition	%	Repetition	%
Quran Sura and supplications	6	24	5	17
Bead	7	28	6	20
Amulet	6	16	6	20
Buzzband	4	12	7	23
Alaq	3	20	6	20
Total	25	100	30	100

We did not find any gypsy person who pays zakat on his money or understands zakat as an obligation in Islam. This is due to ignorance of many religious matters, including this, and the conviction of most of them that most of their actions are contrary to the Islamic religion, and that their sources of financial income come through the forbidden path.

Pilgrimage, as an Islamic religious duty, is not a concern for gypsies in general. Some people talked to me contradictorily about two or three people who had gone on pilgrimage, and some of them repented of the actions of the gypsies and adhered religiously, and some of them remained the same after their return.

When we asked the study sample in the two areas if they knew the position of Islam towards their professions, the answer was:

Table -14- Do you believe that most of your professions are contrary to Islam?

Area	Kamaliya	Fawwar	Total	%
Yes	45	46	100	100
No	-	-	-	-
Total	54	46	100	100

The answers show that the gypsies are fully aware of the position of religion towards most of the actions that they practice, as well as they are contrary to the customs and traditions of our Arab society. Therefore, they became rejected by society. There is no doubt that this awareness resulted from the cultural contact that the various channels of communication provide them with, including direct civil contact with non-gypsies, and the influence of powerful media such as television, radio, and others.

We asked the study sample in the two areas if some gypsies think of leaving their work, most of which is contrary to Islam, as we mentioned.

Table 15- Have you ever thought of quitting your work and adhering to religion?

Area	Kamaliya	%	Fawwar	%
Yes	10	19	15	33
No	44	81	31	67
Total	54	100	46	100

The residents of Kamaliya who thought or are thinking of leaving their jobs that are contrary to religion are very few compared to the study sample and fewer compared to their counterparts in the Fawwar area.

There are several reasons for this, including what we mentioned earlier, because of their constant contact with the wider community in the area (Qadisiya Province), which, as I said, is considered more conservative than the community of the capital, Baghdad. As for the gypsy residents of the Kamaliya, despite their direct and continuous contact with the neighbouring community of non-Gypsies, and their direct neighbourhood relations and the opportunity for more contact. They are less enthusiastic than thinking of leaving their professions. There are several reasons behind that, among which are:

1- Their living requirements are abundant due to their location in Baghdad, the capital, in addition to the difficulties of living due to high prices.

2- They do not have skills, high competence, or educational degrees that qualify them for another job, in addition to the insufficient income from most other professions.

3- They got used to gaining money in easy ways, including fraud on visitors to their areas. This applies to most of the gypsy areas in Iraq.

Conclusion:

1. The gypsies in Iraq follow the Islamic religion, as a kind of social adaptation with which the gypsies have been known in most parts of the world.

2. Gypsies in general do not adhere to the teachings of Islam, and their commitment is only in terms of a transactional aspect of the religion, and that is because they are besieged by it by society and the authority.

3. They also adhere to some rituals and practices, such as visiting holy shrines, taking vows, and others. We believe that this is explained by two aspects, the first of which is social adaptation, and the second is expiatory rituals. [121]

4. Fawwar gypsies are closer to religion, and they practice some of its rituals more than the gypsies of Kamaliya area, due to their location (Fawwar) in a relatively conservative area and being near some holy religious places. This means that Fawwar gypsies are more adapted in this aspect.

---

[121] It is a term developed by the researcher and means the feeling of guilt and reprimand of the individual or the group when they find that their actions are in contrary to religion. These rituals are an expression of remorse by supplication, or making vows or gifts, to atone for guilt.

Chapter Six

Economic System

Mirth (singing, music, and dancing)

Sex trade (sex work and brokering in it)

Commercial business

Other activities

Conclusion

Economic system:

The economic system is concerned with a group's financial activities, or, as Spradley & McCurdy say, it aims to reveal the productive activity of a group of individuals. It aims at producing, distributing, and exchanging goods and services. [122] Therefore, it deals with other activities that are broader and directly related to the economic system.

Sociologists and anthropologists who study economic systems do not look at economic activities in the same way economists do. They look at it from different angles, they are more interested in the social effects of economic aspects, and their efforts are not limited to these effects only, but extend to other aspects that are less clear. For example, they ask, what are the effects of professional specialization on personality? What are the effects of this specialization on educational activity and its impact on family life? How do family orientations grow and change? What drives a person to work after they satisfy their basic needs? [123] and so on.

The economic system is defined as "the extensive study of the activities and events that are related to the utilization of natural wealth resources, and their limitations and uses, which are related to the organisation that is related to the satisfaction of biological and social needs". [124]

---

[122] Ismail, Farouq, Cultural Anthropology, Op. Cit, P. 355.

[123] Ibid, P. 183

[124] Al Bayati, Op. Cit, P, 252.

Gypsies' Main Economical Activities

These activities are considered the most important sources of financial income for gypsies currently. Gypsies practised previous jobs, which are traditional professions known to most gypsies in the world, such as making sieves, baskets, dental implants, and blacksmithing. Some of the nomadic gypsies [125] who are still called the original gypsies, work in some of these professions, especially blacksmithing (the work of blacksmithing and knives and machetes sharpening), moreover, most of the Qarach still practice such professions.

Some points about these activities can be referred to:

1. The most important thing that distinguishes the main economic activities mentioned above, which are practised now, is that they are not desirable as a family profession in general for the Iraqi, Arab and Islamic societies, that's for music, singing and dancing. When it comes to sex work and brokering, it is known that they are forbidden in Islamic Law and the rest of religions. Idiomatically, sex work means illegal sexual intercourse, while brokerage here is the mediation between the two parties in the sexual process, managing it and preparing the appropriate place for it. A similar thing can be applied to the alcoholic drinks trade as their judgement and their drinkers' judgement in Islam are quite the same.

2. These current events are also characterized by the fact that they arose on the ruins of some of the previous gypsies' professions, such as beggary, wandering, and praising using some popular poems accompanied by rebab musical instrument. That is for a small price, which is food for a meal, wheat, uncooked rice, bread,

---

[125] Some gypsies told that to me during the fieldwork study.

and so on. In the past, until recently, in the mid-seventies of this century, the gypsies, men, used to do this work. They arouse the Arabs, especially the tribal sheikhs and notables, taking advantage of the value of generosity that the Arabs are proud of. Many of them may receive more donations and be honoured guests of some of the sheikhs with their families. Their women also do fortune-telling, dentures, and begging.

Since most of their works are like begging, and since they, men, and women, enjoyed the hospitality of the sheikh. Since rural societies segregated males and females by customs, traditions and religion, the opportunity here is favourable for gypsy women to be a subject to flirtation by some sheikhs and their sons as well. They also practice praising through singing which requires boldness. This way, all these works arose to support each other as the need for money and living required begging, which was in a less polite form. It took the form of praise, which required a musical instrument known as rebab, and praise turned into singing, and singing needed dancing flourished with drinking alcohol. There is no doubt that in this last stage and an atmosphere like this, the gypsy women were, abused by others or with the consent of the gypsies themselves. This started in the period before this stage, in the early eighties, as getting a kiss from a gypsy dancer for a price of (a quarter of a dinar) or to sit next to her or removing the scarf or veil from her head for a price like this. This is called (Africa), which means revealing her hair.

These transformations took place after the decline of the previous professions as well, after the advancement that Iraq witnessed during that period, when most of these tools and machines, which we named with others as the gypsies' traditional works, began to be dispensed with.

And when the previous professions were dispensed with, besides the state's endeavour to find stability for the gypsies after it made a settlement for many nomadic Bedouins, it created several gatherings for gypsies from the early seventies to early eighties. These gatherings were named as (Kamaliya, Radwaniya, Abu Ghraib in Baghdad, Abu Tararid, Qadisiya and Al-Tarab neighbourhood in Zubair - Basra, Sahhaji - Mosul, Al Sharaka Al Gharbiya - Samawah, and the Ottomania Al Amiriya, Nasiriyah).

And since the gypsies were not educated and did not have skills for any other available jobs, these professions that we referred to at the beginning began to flourish and become active. They are the professions that were practised in the temples, as we mentioned in a previous chapter (see "Hypotheses in the origin of the gypsies – Al Kawliya).

Types of Economic Activities:

Entertainment (Singing, music, and dancing)

It is one of the main professions on which gypsies rely for their livelihood, and the study showed that many of them work in this profession.

This study agreed with the researcher Taha Hammadi Al-Hadithi's study conducted in 1976, which showed similar results. It showed that the number of people in this field forms 81.8% of the total gypsy productive force. [126]

---

[126] Al Hadithi, Op. Cit, p118.

In the past, singing among the gypsies was mainly accompanied by a rebab which is a traditional musical instrument that appeared in the desert and was usually used by Bedouins. The Rebab manufacturing is simple, it is made from wood or a square plate whose one side only is used as strings of horse tail hair are attached to it, usually extending longitudinally to a fixed wooden arm. An almost semicircular-shaped wooden bow or wire with hair strings of a similar type tied from end to end is used to play the rebab.

Nowadays, musical instruments such as the oud, the violin, and the qanun are used, in addition to the use of folkloric percussion rhythm instruments such as the drum of all kinds (Kheshba, Zinjari, Zanbur, and others).

Gypsy's sons play on these instruments. Skilled non-gypsy musicians are also sometimes hired, especially when recording tapes for sale or important concerts. Gypsy parties are held continuously in their areas as a commercial process, as several singing and dancing parties are held in more than one house and at the same time, in honour of some guests who keep coming frequently to gypsy areas at night times. The customer pays a lot of money for that, as he is served drinks at high prices, and money is also paid for flirting or kissing the dancer or the woman with whom he is sitting.

And the matter may expand to reach sexual intercourse with one of them in a private and prepared place in the house.

The gypsy tradition prohibits the presence of a gypsy as a customer in the house of his neighbour or the gypsy from the area who is conducting the party. Some justified that saying that "If our girls amuse the Arab, [127] then you, the gypsy, how could you come to us as your daughter is dancing?".

This situation can be explained on the basis that low self-esteem [128] is a general feeling among the gypsies of the low status of this job, and a feeling of inferiority even towards each other. These reactions are interpreted as having equal prestige. Singing parties are called (Dag and Ragus) which means (play and dance). [129]

The gypsy family relies a lot on its daughters because of the nature of this profession, as it mainly depends on the woman, and therefore you find many families depend on their women to support them, and for this reason the delay in the age of marriage for the gypsy girl can be noticed to an exceed 25 years old. [130] This reliance on women was also a reason for the high dowry in the gypsy communities.

The involvement of children begins at a young age in these activities. We surveyed a sample of 18 female and male students from Al-Islah primary school in the gypsy village of Fawwar. We found out that (six) of them said that they were involved at the age of (eight years) in this family business such as dancing, singing, and playing on musical instruments.

---

[127] "Arab", for the gypsies, refers to the non-gypsy person and he is also called "Kaji" in their language.

[128] Al Nuri, Qais, Family as a developmental project, Cultural affairs House, Baghdad, 1994, page number is missing.

[129] The word "Dag" means "playing" which is originally taken from playing drums.

[130] Spinsterhood and the late age of marriage for young Iraqis of both genders have become a general phenomenon due to the successive wars and the circumstances of the blockade against the country.

Involving children in a family business is of great importance for the gypsies, resulting from deepening the love of this profession in them and making them acquire the skill through practising starting from an early age. Since they know that their sons could be involved in other jobs depending on their educational levels, gypsy families prefer their sons to quit school and join the family business. They form 60% of the study sample, which is (100 families) in both study areas; (54 families in Kamaliya, and 46 families in Fawwar).

The study showed that the percentage of those who would like their children to complete their education in the Fawwar area is lower than that of the heads of families in the Kamaliya area. We see that another reason can be added to the reasons mentioned earlier which is that secondary schools are far away from the Fawwar area, unlike the Kamaliya area, as it is in Baghdad, the capital, in which all school types and stages are available, and therefore school costs are lower. We can also notice that the gypsies in Kamaliya have more opportunities for communication, contact, and knowledge in Baghdad. Nevertheless, we cannot ignore illiteracy that prevails in the gypsy community in general.

The gypsies have little association with official and unofficial cultural institutions until recently, and their participation is almost limited to conducting parties on official and unofficial occasions, they sometimes perform at their parties with well-known non-gypsy bands and singers.

Gypsies prefer to cooperate with non-gypsy artistic bands; it occurred only a few times. The reasons behind that, as we see, are that they fear others' exploitation and harassment because of the way people look at gypsies, and due to the gypsy's lack of culture and their fear of not keeping up with others in musical culture and other fields. [131]

Note that the sources of lyrics sung by gypsies, music and melodies all belong to non-gypsies. We investigated a large group of musical tapes of gypsy singers and found out that all the melodies were previously heard and sung by Iraqi and Arab singers or unknown country singers and recordings.

We also obtained similar information from gypsy and non-gypsy people during the fieldwork study. There are many young people who visit gypsy areas frequently, and they have singing talents which are known among gypsies. They recorded parties and singing tapes in association with the gypsies in their areas.

Singing profession is associated with the gypsies in our society and in the folklore heritage. A proverb is often said as: (A wedding at Al Kawliya), This proverb is set for those who master a work, craftsmanship or a talent. A favourable opportunity comes to show it and devote to it, as we indicated in another place.

---

[131] It should not be neglected that the Baghdad commercial theatres attract some gypsy female singers and put them in seductive, singing and dancing roles whose purpose is to attract the audience, as it is well known.

Table -16- Economic activities of the families' heads in both study areas.

Area / Profession	Kamaliya Male	Kamaliya Female	Kamaliya Total	Kamaliya %	Fawwar Male	Fawwar Female	Fawwar Total	Fawwar %
Musician	10	-	10	19	7	-	7	15
Singer	5	2	7	13	4	3	7	15
Female dancer	-	3	3	6	-	3	3	7
Sex work and brokering in it	3	2	5	9	2	1	3	7
Shop managing	5	-	5	9	8	3	11	23
Driver	6	-	6	11	7	-	7	11
Disabled	4	-	4	7	3	-	3	7
Housewife	-	6	6	11	-	1	1	7
Unemployed	6	-	6	11	4	-	4	11
Unspecified	2	-	2	4	-	-	-	-
Total	41	13	54	100	35	11	46	100

The previous table made it clear that the profession of mirth with its branches (music, singing and dancing) ranked first by its practitioners among the heads of families in both study areas. Managing a commercial or alcoholic beverages shop came second in the Fawwar area. In comparison with the Kamaliya area, we find that there are only (5 individuals) of family heads and males who practice this profession, due to the restrictions imposed on the process of opening a shop in the residential area in Kamaliya and the presence of shops and commercial streets close to it.

We also find that three women are heads of families in Fawwar, each one of them runs a store. This is a natural issue with no negative side, as is the case in neighbouring areas or Iraq in general.

Sex Trade [132]

As soon as the word gypsy or kawli is uttered in front of a person in Iraq, two main things come to that person's mind: mirth (dancing, singing, and music) and sex (adultery).

Earlier, we mentioned the reasons that prompted gypsies to these two professions.

They can be summarized as follows:
1- The decline of the previous traditional professions because people dispensing with them because of technological progress..

---

[132] A term developed by the author to refer to the process of organising and managing illegal sex to benefit financially and to be taken as a profession.

2- When this decline occurred and due to the intensity of life's demands, the gypsies focused their efforts on mirth as a profession, because they had experience in it resulting from wandering and praising people on the melodies of the rebab.

3- The gathering of gypsies in isolated areas (ghettoes), the continuous demand by the public for them to perform at parties to satisfy the desires of mirth lovers, and money flow, all encouraged them to do so.

4- Mirth atmosphere is commonly accompanied by alcoholic beverage consumption, and this led to more deviation, especially in a mixed atmosphere when men and women are all together, with the presence of female singers and dancers.

5- The atmosphere of mirth in such circumstances leads to (a lack of modesty), and as the popular proverb says (singing reduces modesty), and thus, such phenomena leaking into the souls is quite possible.

6- The isolation of these areas and the availability of space for such acts made them places of refuge and shelter for delinquents, deviants, and expatriates from their reality, including sex workers and non-gypsy sinners.

We believe here that the best explanation for what happened to this status of the gypsies is the explanation provided by the functionalist school represented by the anthropologist Malinowski: "as a kind of adaptation carried out by society in line with the development of life, justifying this by the fact that the human being is characterized by a high ability to adapt and be compatible with it and organise ways to satisfy those motives in a very precise and tidily way". [133]

---

[133] Mahjoub, Mohamed Abdou, An Introduction to the Socio-anthropological Direction, The Egyptian Book Organisation, Alexandria, 1977, P. 189.

It is represented by satisfying the sexual drive through marriage, and Malinowski sees culture as "how the human being satisfies his various needs'. [134]

When you ask the gypsy about sex trade and its legitimacy or something else about it, he says (our daughters do not do this, and these sex workers are not gypsies, but they come running away from their reality because of committing a sin that is difficult to fix such as defloration of the virginity before marriage. So she fears the punishment of her family and remains here. The other reason for seeking shelter is either she lost her family or the ones who embrace her, or it is her way of living.) We know stories of women who were forced by need to follow this path.

Many gypsy families, in all known gypsy areas, have embraced one or more non-gypsy girls who usually have good aesthetic qualities, and a brokerage process takes place in exchange for money from people who frequently visit the gypsy areas. The amount starts with (25 dinars, which is equal to one dollar) and is graded according to the woman/ beauty and age. The family that runs this process allocates a small cottage or a private room and a modest mattress, but the place is usually neither clean nor healthy.

The customer at the door (the door of the house) agrees with a man or woman who organises the entry and exit process and takes the price himself/herself. This person is called (the procurer), this procurer is either from the people of this house or an employee. In this case, he is a stranger to the area of the course (either a person who became a gypsy or ran away from his/her reality and love the

---

[134] Ibid, P. 189.

life of the gypsies, or from the foreigners working in the country). The duty of the procurer begins with fulfilling some of the needs of the house, such as shopping. Then he/she stands at the door of the house calling out to passers-by in a way that looks like (promotion) in a way of enticement and takes the price to delivers it to the people of the house. His work extends to protecting the sex worker from assault or abuse by clients or defrauding them as well, or he plays the role of the mobster (bully) is to protect the girl.

Scams, fraud, and misrepresentation of customers do occur, and we happened to witness many cases like this to many customers during the fieldwork study. Girls expose themselves in loose clothes and seductive words and positions to passers-by customers, and sometimes with entreaties. Some of them do not expose themselves unless the client stipulates to see her. They expose themselves with great reservation because most of the sex workers working here if they are not gypsies, are either runaways and settled here for reasons we mentioned previously or girls who spend days or hours and then return. During this short period, the purpose is either to satisfy the sexual pleasure that they lack in their homes for the reasons of (the husbands' absence or negligence) or to receive an amount of money due to financial need.

These women are very careful not to easily reveal their identities or their faces in the street or the area. Bringing such women to the area is arranged through secret, organised and accurate operations far from the eyes of the public and the security services. There are gypsies' houses in the middle of the cities and major neighbourhoods. These houses attract women in different ways through gypsy women or men or those who deal with the gypsies. Then, those women keep visiting these houses frequently. Activities that can be called a white slave trade take place. A police officer told me that a gypsy woman was arrested with another woman who ran away from her family. The police officer learned that she had been sold more than once among gypsies for brokering. It was difficult for her to return, fearing the punishment of her family, as she stayed with the gypsies, and she's been, by her will, to more than one gypsy area.

This illegal sex activity is called in the region (Winssa) which means enjoyment.

The gypsy here does not feel embarrassed when he manages or supervises such work or when it happens in his house, but when he goes outside the circle of his area, the opposite happens and he tries to justify with various justifications, including saying that the gypsies want to live.

His behaviour and feelings in his area and with people of his race (Gypsies), when he does not feel embarrassed, are the result of the fact that society behaves similarly and that everyone understands his condition and circumstances, which generally apply to everyone.

Gypsies are accused of kidnapping young non-Gypsy girls to prepare them for future jobs such as dancing, singing, sex work or marriage. We did not confirm this from police stations or see such cases.

Table -17- The ratio of homes that conduct sex work (Winssa) to the whole sample in both study areas.

Area	Kamaliya	%	Fawwar	%	Total
Available	23	43	24	52	47
Unavailable	31	57	22	48	53
Total	54	100	46	100	100

We noticed from the previous table that 43-52% of houses in the Fawwar area conduct sex work compared to the Kamaliya area. We believe that it is due to the fear and reservation of the Kamaliya gypsies, and their extreme caution against the police patrols that sometimes raid them for any reason (as violations occur a lot in the area and the gypsy areas in general), besides the fact that the area is no more than small open neighbourhood and several houses located within a large residential area. This fact causes them problems with the neighbouring people of the area because their actions conflict with religion, customs, and traditions, as we mentioned earlier. They also fear that the sex workers' families will attack and kill them and other similar problems. For all those reasons, and to avoid such attacks, the houses' owners use some tricks which are known to most constant visitors such as:

- Writing the phrase (the house is for sale, contact the owner of the house) on the outer wall of the house.
- Writing the phrase (House of Arabs) it is known that the gypsies call the public (non-gypsies) (Arabs).

Thus, it is a way to avoid any trouble with the police or others claiming to be an Arab house and have nothing to do with sex work. Nevertheless, we learned that there are no such Arab houses within the gypsy area as most people have sold their homes there to avoid suspicion and problems. In addition, these camouflage phrases and methods do not exist in any other gypsy area, except for Kamaliya, due to the specificity of its location as we mentioned earlier.

What is happening here concerning the sex trade is fully applicable to the interpretation of the exchange theory, as it begins with a social interaction between two parties (the sex worker who comes or is brought to the area - the gypsies - and the gypsy family that embraces her or the broker who organises work on her) to be an exchange of benefits. He exploits her as an investment project, so that the third party (the customer) takes part in the process.

Homans' equation [135] in the theory of social exchange can be applied to explain the social relations among people. The first party is the sex worker who comes to seek financial reward or someone who provides shelter for her. The second party is the broker, who is rewarded with the money that he will cut from the wages that the customer pays (who becomes the third party). The cost paid by the second party (the broker) is the adaptation, effort, responsibility, and risk that he bears because of his work. The third party (the customer) needs the second party (the broker) to provide him with assistance, which is mediation (brokerage).

To clarify the concepts (cost, profit, and reward) for each of the three parties, we use the following:

---

[135] Zeitlin, already mentioned, p121.

Table -18, cost, profit, and reward of the sex work parties.

	Profit	Rewards	Cost
The second party*	Cut from wage	Full wage from the customer	Shelter + effort + responsibility + risk
The first party	Wage + sexual pleasure	Wage + pleasure + shelter	Risk + loss of reputation
The third party	Sexual pleasure	Pleasure + facilitation	Money

*Note: "Second party" refers to the broker, "Third party" refers to the sex worker and the "Third party" refers to the customer.

These relationships can be called the primary processes among people as referred to by Peter Blau as achieving a better understanding of the evolution of the complex structures of the correlations that bind people.[136]

(Lack of balance, inconsistency, and dependency on one side) may appear in this type of relationship. It is called a mini relationship due to the entry of the power dimension into the social exchange. The strength here is the ability to enforce and sustain compliance through negative sanctions. This applies to the broker's relationship with the sex worker, which is sometimes characterized by the control of the first and the acquiescence of the second.

---

[136] Zeitlin, p142

The Commercial Business

This activity includes opening and owning commercial shops usually located in the gypsy area, and these shops are established on the sidelines of the gypsy life and its activities (in other words, they meet the needs of the area according to their lifestyle and requirements).

Most of them sell alcoholic beverages, due to the community's need for them here, because of the nature of life, as the atmosphere of joy requires that, in addition to the absence of social controls over that, even a child can consume these drinks without deterrence or supervision. Most families may involve their children in drinking, and the only reason for preventing them would be to save drinks due to their lack. We surveyed the opinions of primary school students in the gypsy area in Fawwar, and everyone answered that if someone is prevented from consuming a drink, the reason would be to save drinks. Children usually drink what is left of the alcohol in glasses.

There are small shop-size bars, where buyer can sit and have his drink or take it with him (seferi). Usually, the seller in such bars is a girl to attract customers.

Sanitary paper (Kleenex), shampoo, toiletry items, washing powders, ice and cigarettes are among the commodities that are compatible with the nature of life and fill a need. These items are sold at very high prices, some of which may be twice the official price in nearby cities.

The matter of opening a commercial store attached to the house is very easy in the Fawwar area, and we knew this through the fieldwork study, as there were many shops there. We obtained statistics for the number of commercial stores dating back to the year 1987. [137] The statistics told us that there were 95 commercial stores there, which were either for selling liquor or bars or any other commercial stores.

The ease of opening shops is since the area is not subject to commercial supervision and its conditions, and the area is far from the city (the nearest city is the city of Diwaniyah, approximately 12 km).

As for the Kamaliya area, unlike Fawwar, it is subject to commercial supervision and conditions for opening stores. Therefore, this phenomenon almost disappears in Baghdad, except for small windows or tables selling cigarettes (chamber) at the door of the house.

The following table shows the price differences in the gypsy area and the official prices in other cities.

Table -19 Price differences* in the gypsy areas compared to city prices up to June 1994.

Item	Unit	Official price	Price in gypsy areas
Electric bulb	1	70	150
Sumer cigarettes packet	One packet	70	150
Sumer cigarette	One cigarette	5	10
Bear bottle	One bottle	75	100
Whisky	One bottle	300	400
Wine	One bottle	150	200
Cloth washing liquid	One bottle	50	200
Cloth washing powder	One packet	60	80
Tissue paper	One packet	10	25
Ice	One ice mould	10	100

---

[137] Ministry of Planning's sources.

* (Prices are in Iraqi dinar whose value, at that time, was 50 dinars for one dollar)

These prices represent the reality and the situation that the Fawwar area and all other gypsy areas in Iraq suffer from. This suffering is exacerbated by the fact that the gypsies bring their rations of foodstuffs organised by the government from food agents in the cities near them. The competent authorities did not grant them an agency, not even to any of the shop owners in their areas.

Among the reasons for the high prices are:
1. The area is relatively far from the city, as we mentioned, and this means that transportation charges are added to the prices.
2. There are no food and other agencies supported by the government.
3. Absence of commercial supervision.
4. Weak religious and moral thinking.

From observing the main economic activities prevailing today, we see that the rise or fall of the living condition of any gypsy family depends mainly on the presence of young and beautiful female members in the family. It is not an essential condition for the talent of singing or dancing, and if there is any, that is the best for her of course.

And just as the income of some gypsy families is very high, their requirements are too many. There is a big difference in the nature of housing between the two study areas in Kamaliya and Fawwar, in terms of ownership, the type of housing and its relationship to the area, and other data that will be presented by the following tables, each one of them is followed by analysis.

Table – 20 – House types' relation to the area.

House type	Bricks	Clay	Tent	Wicker	Other	Total
Kamaliya	217	-	-	-	-	217
%	100	-	-	-	-	100
Fawwar	210	5	2	3	-	220
%	95,4	2,2	1	1,3	-	100

All gypsy houses in Kamaliya are built with bricks, according to modern plans and construction. This is a result of the high economic situation of the families there in general, and the influence of the housing style in Baghdad as well as the urban planning of the city of Baghdad. This urban planning requires a commitment to the building according to a building plan and the details of the main and secondary streets and the availability of services and building supplies. In addition, ownership of these houses (Real Estate Registration) plays a role here as the house's ownership is officially registered. On the contrary, in Fawwar area the land is still not owned by gypsies, but it is considered (an encroachment) and (Al Mithl) is collected from them, which is (a tax deducted in favour of the governmental Real Estate Department). [138]

---

[138] Diwaniyah Mayor Office, with editor Mr. Fahim on April 30th, 1994.

Table -21- shows ownership and its relation to the area.

Ownership	Owned	Rented	Governmental	Other	Total
Kamaliya	173	44	-	-	217
%	80	20	-	-	100
Fawwar	220	-	-	-	220
%	100	-	-	-	100
Total	393	44	-	-	437
%	90	10	-	-	100

The above table shows that (44) houses are rented by the gypsies in the Kamaliya area, and this means several things, including:

1. This adds more economic burdens to some gypsy families in Kamaliya, especially if we compare the percentage of high house rent prices since the area is in Baghdad, the capital.
2. This means an increase in the standards of living in the Kamaliya area through better job opportunities and higher wages due to its location in Baghdad, which led to an increase in migration to it.
3. This also means the existence of shared housing for several families, whether related or not, to reduce the economic burdens.

Table – 22- shows the facilities available in the house as a comparison between both study areas.

Available facilities	Bath	Toilet	Electricity	Water	Telephone	Garden	Other
Kamaliya	217	217	217	217	100	100	-
%	100	100	100	100	46	46	-
Fawwar	100	200	210	-	-	-	-
%	44	88	92	-	-	-	-

This data reveals, in a simple comparison, the extent of the difference in terms of services available in the two study areas. If we know that the services mentioned above, if available, provide a good living environment to reduce the economic burdens on the family. They represent an important factor that helps in social adaptation by keeping pace with the wider community and reducing physical and psychological differences as well.

Other Economic Activities

They are represented in a group of activities, the most important of which is (taxi driving), repairing, buying, and selling some musical instruments.

Car driving is a favourite profession for gypsies because it meets more of their needs and prevents them from the greed of other drivers. Generally, there are very few gypsies who can buy a private car or a taxi. And as we learned, gypsies, despite their high incomes, do not save money, for reasons like many living requirements and ways of spending, such as gambling, as many of them resort to gambling and extravagance. During the fieldwork study, we saw several manifestations of gambling, including playing cards or participating in horse competitions (races) and cockfighting bets. Among the reasons for not saving is their many problems, The solution for most of those problems requires spending money and even settling down their own disputes, besides their lack of commercial sense and their lack of confidence in whoever it is necessary to cooperate with to invest their money. This does not preclude saying that some of them have owned real estate and invested their money in good projects, and this applies especially to some of Kamaliya's gypsies.

Stratification almost disappears in the gypsy society, in terms of the economic situation, as the gypsy area in Kamaliya is characterized by a better economic situation and good services by virtue of its location in Baghdad. In the same area, there are some houses whose construction and furnishings indicate a high financial state and a better status, such as the house of Sheikh Nimr's sons (Mohammed and Ghadban).

The comparison shows the lack of services in the Fawwar area compared to the Kamaliya, for many reasons, the most prominent of which are:
1. Kamaliya area, which is now located within the borders of the Municipality of Baghdad, is of great importance and must be cared for like the rest of the capital's regions, unlike Fawwar area, which is isolated (12 km) far from the city of Diwaniyah, the centre of Qadisiya Governorate.
2. The Kamaliya gypsy area is located within an inhabited geographic area, the gypsies share it with the rest of the population of Arab people (as called by the gypsies), and only a ten-meter-wide street separates them from Arabs.

The gypsy residents of Kamaliya area can be distinguished by their high level of financial income compared to other gypsy areas, including Fawwar but credibility is almost absent in the respondents' answers due to the study community's fear of giving correct data, as they distrust strangers. They feel afraid because most of what they do is illegal and many of their problems come from their visitors. As a result, wage instability and work irregularity, due to its nature, can be noticed. But in general, the level of monthly income in the Kamaliya area is higher than it is in Fawwar, because of its location in Baghdad, which means many people come to visit them. This huge number of visitors is due to the large population density of Baghdad, the anonymity that dominates its society, the community's openness, many job opportunities, including many nightclubs, and Baghdad's high standards of living.

Talents in singing and dancing appear among the gypsies, so they migrate to Baghdad for a better income, in addition to the opportunities of appearing in the media and recording studios that record tapes for them and print their pictures.

The fieldwork study data showed a high cost of living in the Kamaliya area compared to other gypsy areas, including Fawwar in Qadisiya Governorate. This is due to several reasons including the large number of life requirements in an area located in the capital, in addition to the high prices in Baghdad, which are higher than those in Qadisiya Governorate taking into consideration some things that contradict this interpretation. For instance, the failure to deliver clear water through pipes to the gypsy area in Fawwar has led to an increase in the costs spent for this purpose, as water is delivered by tanker trucks to the village and is sold at very high prices (for example, filling a medium-sized water tank for the house is equivalent to approximately one dollar) and is only fairly enough to two-day domestic use. As for bathing, most of the residents can't do it in their homes, so the people of the area go to nearby towns, especially the town of Afak, which is about 20 km away from the village. In Afak, there is a large public bath in which there are two days for women, Mondays and Thursdays and we noticed that the gypsy women keep coming to this bath.

The lack of piped water delivery to this area caused great suffering to its people and weakened the cost of living, as well as a reason to make it a population-expulsing area after it was recently a polarizing area.

Spending on bathing and make-up is very necessary for gypsy women because they are related to their professions. Sitting with male clients (Al Kayafa), [139] as the gypsies call them. Dancing, singing, or sitting in a shop or an alcoholic beverage shop requires cleanliness and a beautiful appearance.

In transportation comparison, we notice the difference more obvious in Kamaliya area due to its closeness to Baghdad and the availability of transportation means, unlike the isolated area of Fawwar, which is not connected by a direct road line except for saloon taxis operating on a line with a fee that reached (what is equivalent of half a dollar) to travel between Diwaniyah and the village. But the reason for this is that Kamaliya gypsies keep frequently and constantly coming to the areas of Baghdad.

The economic difference between the gypsy area in Kamaliya appears as a pattern of gypsy settlement and other gatherings, as this is a result of the high income in the Kamaliya area resulting from the availability of job opportunities there. Having more such furniture

---

[139] It is a colloquial word in the Iraqi dialect, and it is taken from the word (kaif), which means a pleasant mood and psychological comfort, and this word is used to describe singing and mirth.

means getting closer to the wider society and symmetrizing with it and adapting to technology.

The availability of devices, such as television, which is the most important media device, is an important factor in influencing and directing any society. The abundance of television and radio appliances means that we can control, as much as possible, directing and delivering the government plans and policies, as well as delivering the national character and symbols of civilization, and eliminating cultural differences among subcultures.

What we saw during the fieldwork study in the Fawwar area was the use of the traditional clay oven, which is a good economic aspect for some families. It saves them from buying cooking gas bottles that are sometimes sold at high prices (equivalent to half a dollar) in their area. With the clay oven, firewood is used, which is brought at no cost from the neighbouring agricultural areas.

Conclusion:

From a comprehensive look at the economic activities, we can draw a brief conclusion, as follows:
1. Most of the gypsies' economic activities are undesirable by the Iraqi society, and most of them are against Sharia, law and custom.
2. They were not productive, and they didn't meet food needs or clothing or supply the market, but rather they were consumption, and entertainment services.
3. The gypsies' financial incomes are large, but their requirements and expenditures are also large. Therefore, we can see the absence

of economic-based stratification in their society, especially in the Fawwar area.

4. The gypsies' economy is characterized by great risk, as it is dependent on many circumstances that may affect it, including government policy and social conditions. In addition, they do not have scientific skills or competencies that qualify them to quickly transform their professions.

5. The gypsy family sometimes depends on one person for its economy, and that is why we see a high rate of unemployment.

6. The gypsy economy depends mainly on women because of the nature of their economic activities.

The most important effects of the economic relationship of the gypsies' activities on the social structure of their society can be summarized as follows:

1. Working in a profession that is despised by others makes a person despise him/herself and look down on him/herself, especially when he/she is living among them. This is called what we mentioned above, low self-esteem, which has many repercussions, including immersion and attachment to his culture, and thus slow social adaptation.

2. The purely material relationships, which almost cover even the relationships of the children of the same family, lead to the development of a restless and alienated personality in many cases.

3. These main economic activities (mirth, sex trade, dealing in alcoholic beverages) that take place in the family milieu mean that all members of the family are aware of them, even the children, and it means that they are informed of the reality of their families. Therefore, either these children are affected by their families and their work, or they create intersections with their families. Both are

big problems. The nature of the practice of such economic activities, which are generally characterized by constant preoccupation, indifference, lack of responsibility and guilt if society rejects them, all of this leads to family disintegration. We noticed a lack of interest in children, especially boys, while the girl received special care to rehabilitate her in the future to be successful in the field of musical arts. We also noticed the negligence of the elderly and the infirm by their families, and this matter is a result of the weakness of human relations. He also noticed that the status of the person and his/her care, even in the same family, depends on what he offers of giving or material return, which confirms point (2) from the above and what was stipulated in the exchange theory.

Chapter Seven

Social control in the gypsy community

Sources of control in the gypsy community:

1. Law (the police)

2. Religion

3. Mores, clan sanctions

Social Control:

Social control is of great importance in understanding and comprehending any society that is to be studied, which is why it can be seen in almost every study of any society. Social control can be defined as "it is an important focal point for sociology today. Some researchers' interest in it reached the point that they imagine that all issues of sociology can be included under this topic, despite the great exaggeration in this opinion". [140]

This term (social control) is used in the social theory part that is concerned with studying methods of maintaining order and stability. Or it may be used in its narrow sense, which refers to the specialized means that are used to maintain order, such as laws, courts, security forces and the police. Sometimes it is used in the study of social foundations and their relationship to one another while they are maintaining social stability, and those foundations are the legitimate, religious, and political ones. [141]

The gypsy groups in Iraq are considered by the rest of the Iraqi society to be out of law, custom and religion. So if they are outside the scope of general social control, how do we view them and how do we study social control? Do we study it on the basis that they are part of the Iraqi society and what applies to it applies to them, or do we study control as a sub-culture with the rest of the systems to form a sub-culture in the comprehensive culture of the Iraqi society?

---

[140] Al-Khashab, Ahmed, Social Control: Its Foundations and Practice, Cairo Bookshop, 1968, p. 19.

[141] Dinken, Michelle, Dictionary of Sociology, translated by Ihsan Al-Hassan, Dar Al-Rashid, Baghdad, 1980, p. 281.

Studying that will be comprehensive and reconciling between the two views based on their subordination and not being isolated from building the totalitarian society viewing them as a distinct sub-culture.

How does the gypsy community deal with things? Are there systems that control it? Behavioural rules? Control means? Or is it a chaotic society if most of its professions are outside the law, Sharia and the rules of the totalitarian society (the society of the Iraqi state that embraces this group)?

There is no doubt that there is no society on the face of the earth that does not have rules and systems that control it. Even if there is such a kind of society, it should have its controlling means which are also primitive and simple and should organise its life and help it keep its entity and the social structure that distinguishes it. This has been confirmed by anthropological studies carried out by anthropologists such as (Malinowski, Evan Pritchard, Lucy Mair, Margaret Mead, Radcliffe Brown, and others) on very primitive and simple societies concerning their way of life. They studied even the societies that were completely isolated from the world, until recently, in isolated places in the middle of the African jungle, the Indian Ocean, the Pacific Ocean, and the Arctic).

The main social control sources in the gypsy community are:

First: Law authority (police):

It is the intense fear of the policemen, and there is no doubt that this is due to several reasons, which are:

- Police officers treat the gypsies with extreme cruelty, and that is a result of the idea they hold about them being out of the law, Sharia and custom.
- Lots of violations and problems occur in the gypsy areas.
- They believe that the police are the strongest authority, and their solutions are superior to other parties, such as the clan council, Al-Mukhtar, or others.

The gypsy individual here understands the law to be mere (the police). What he fears from the police are (physical punishment, imprisonment, fines, stripping him of some of his illegal things such as possession of an unlicensed weapon, or even the fear of being caught sheltering a sex worker. So she will be taken from him and then he will be punished for that.)

The gypsies' problems are many, as we mentioned, and they result from the nature of their professions, the people's perception of them, and the fact that some of their visitors are either outlaws, or they make problems for them because of drunkenness and other things.

There are many gypsy lawsuits in police stations. They are either among the gypsies themselves which range from the simplest things, such as disagreement over some matters to quarrels, divorce problems, sales violations, women-related problems, drinking alcohol and mirth parties, problems because of neighbourly relations or kinship or affinity, or these problems are with others who frequently visit or deal with them, whether in the city or their areas.

It is a natural and very normal thing for problems to occur in any society and to reach police stations. But to be in an excessive number is not normal, that's the situation in the gypsy areas as officials in the police stations are responsible for both study areas told me. Before registering gypsies as Iraqi citizens, they were referred to as (a kawili or a gajari) in the police records, and it was possible to easily count or identify gypsy cases. But now, after being granted citizenship and treated as Iraqi, it is difficult to search the police records to decide if the case belongs to a gypsy or others. It can only be identified when the case's type is known.

The large number of lawsuits filed with the police compared to the problems of the public (non-gypsies) indicates matters that can be summarized as follows:

1. Deviation of most of the inhabitants of this community from the law, religion, and social custom prevailing in the large society, which is either represented by some of their professions or the behaviours and actions that result from them.
2. The weakness of their internal social control factors.
3. Their poor adaptation or the difficulty of being accepted by other people.

Table 23- represents the party or means of control that gypsies reckon with more than others.

Area	Police	Religion	Tribe	Criticizing others	Total
Kamaliya	49	3	1	1	54
%	90.7	5.5	1.8	1.8	100
Fawwar	35	6	5	-	46
%	76	13	11	-	100

The fieldwork study data shows that the police are the party that is most reckoned with by the gypsies in both areas. The reason for that, as we see it, is due to the weakness of the other control factors in comparison with the police force and their influence on them besides knowing some penalties imposed by the police on violators.

Table 24- shows some penalties and sentences issued against members of the sample families.

Sentence / Area	Death	Prison	Custody	Fine	Other	Total
Kamaliya	4	18	25	-	-	56
%	7	33	46	17	-	
Fawwar	3	10	13	7	-	33
%	6.5	22	28	15	-	

Comparing the range of punishments, the data of which was obtained from the study sample of families in both study areas, shows that the percentage is higher in Kamaliya area than it is in Fawwar. The reason for that is the large number of problems in it (Kamaliya) because of its location in Baghdad, which has a high population density. The gypsy housing area there is in direct contact with non-gypsies which leads to many accidents. In addition, the police station is near the area, as a result, arresting or searching for the perpetrator becomes easy. On the contrary, the nearest police station situation in Fawwar area, is (Al-Nahda neighbourhood police station) in Diwaniyah, which is about (15 km) away.

These sentences and penalties have a major role in controlling the behaviour of individuals, which is what makes them reckon more with the police. We learned during the fieldwork study that these sentences came as a result when some of them committed major crimes, including premeditated murder, kidnapping, evading military service, assault, or theft, the simplest of which is a driving violation.

Second: Religion:

It comes second as a controlling factor in the gypsy areas. Despite the apparent interest sometimes in some religious rituals, it is not considered a major control factor in their lives, and we have explained this in "The Religious Pattern" chapter.

The interview form showed a variety of responses to some of the questions that were asked, and these are the data tables:

Table 25- shows whether the studied individual looks at the actions that he performs according to the principle of halal (permitted) or haram (forbidden).

Area	Yes	No	Total
Kamaliya	15	39	54
%	28	72	100
Fawwar	20	26	46
%	43	57	100

The above data shows that those who have a view of the work they do according to the halal and haram principles are generally less than half of the research sample in both areas of Kamaliya and Fawwar. In Kamaliya, we see that the percentage is small, which is (28%) of the research sample, representing (54 families). This percentage is less than its counterpart in the Fawwar gypsy area, which reached (43%), and it is generally less than half of the sample for this area as well.

As I mentioned earlier (see "The religious pattern" chapter), the explanation for this difference is that Fawwar area is in an area that is relatively close to the holy places in Karbala, Najaf, and Kufa, and in a relatively conservative society compared to the broad society of Baghdad, the capital, to which Kamaliya is near. In addition, Fawwar gypsies frequently visit these holy places as a kind of adaptation to the large (totalitarian) society. It also means the majority's ignorance and disregard of these religious principles.

The gypsies, like their popular social milieu, resort to swearing. The oath and it is called (hilf) is one of the important factors of social control, especially among the gypsies. And the oath at the shrines of religious figures and imams is the most important reference for all the problems that require an oath to be resolved. If the matter reaches this stage, the gypsies concerned prepare, wash, and purify themselves, and go to one of the shrines of imams, especially the shrine of Imam Al-Abbas bin Abi Talib in Karbala, and they take the oath there. The gypsies in this situation are more afraid and fearful because they are convinced that God will harm them because of the status of Al-Abbas for Him and they call him (Al-Abbas Abu Ras Al-Har) meaning that he is quick to get angry when someone swears in his name falsely.

Gypsies from most of the gypsy areas go to this place, especially from Fawwar. In Kamaliya, they go to the shrine of Imam Al Kadhim in Baghdad, if they do not go to Karbala or Najaf.

Most of the gypsies in Iraq believe in metaphysical matters that are unseen from the scientific point of view, including what is known as (shara) [142] or (bakhat).

As in many religious societies as well as the societies that rely on metaphysics in their life (non-secular), many beliefs control their behaviour in certain aspects of life, for example, "Mana for the Polynesians and Melanesians" [143] and "karama" for the Egyptians, and others.

We found that the gypsies, especially in the Fawwar area, fear the metaphysical power, "shara", of the Prophet Mohammed's descendants, "sada", and never harm them, even verbally. After surveying the research sample, the above results appeared and showed the discrepancy between the two study areas. The reasons that explain this were explained in the explanation of the previous similar tables in this chapter.

Although no "sada", Prophet Mohammed's descendants or those who have "shara" or "bakhat", live among the gypsies, they avoid them, and we believe that this is generally a result of their frequent visits to the holy shrines. We also believe that it is complementary to the expiatory rituals.

---

[142] It means the power that a person of high religious status possesses, which God bestows on him for his piety and asceticism, or for his lineage - like the gentlemen who are descended from the lineage of Ali bin Abi Talib and his wife Fatima, daughter of the Prophet Mohammad - and shara - here is a parapsychological or supernatural ability to harm those who harm or offend them.

[143] Mair, Lucy, Op. Cit, p464.

What we noticed also is the severity of exaggeration in this aspect, as (they swear by some Prophet Mohammed's descendants "sada", such as Sayed Malik, who is still alive and lives in Numaniyah, Wasit Governorate and has a good status and fame in this aspect).

Third: Norms

It is a set of behavioural models that must be adhered to by members of society because of their great traditional and social importance. [144]

Norms are an important tool of social control, and they represent the small circle of the sub-culture of society and the customs, traditions, and values that it follows to preserve the social structure and its general internal entity.

The norms of the gypsy community are the other internal controls that determine and restrict this community members' behaviour besides the other tools of control (law and religion) that were mentioned earlier and that are related to the customs, values, and traditions of this community.

If a person behaves contrary to the behaviour of their society, we find that the deterrent comes to them either through an external or internal force. The external represents the law, religion, or general mores (such as the tribal council, family, or public opinion). While the internal force from the same person is what we call remorse.

---

[144] Ibid, p. 464.

We saw at the beginning of this chapter and in table (40) that mores (which we classified under "criticizing others") came in third place, according to the gypsies, as a means of social control.

The gypsy society has mores that are a tool of control, but they are weak in extending their influence and sway over their members. When a gypsy individual violates those mores, the gypsy community has no serious reaction to deter him/her compared to what it did in the past, that's for the following reasons:

1. The gypsy society is in a phase of degeneration of its social and moral structure.
2. The openness of the gypsy community (as a sub-culture) to the broader totalitarian society (Iraqi society), led to the gypsies becoming aware of the reality of their position in the dominant culture and that their culture is characterized by some values that collide with the values and standards of the wider society. This matter exposes them to social rejection or ostracism, and this is a general rule [145] and their culture can be called an intersectional culture.
3. The family disintegration experienced by the gypsy family due to the nature of its professions.

The following table shows the gypsy family members' practices of some acts that are abnormal and undesirable according to the general attitude. However, they declared themselves as well. Those practices lead to deviation, to health and economic harms, and to breach public mores and as those practices are adopted by most of their elders.

---

[145] See Al Nouri, Qais, Subcultures and the Problematic Professional Development in the Arabian Gulf, Journal of Arab Studies, Issue 4, year 29, January - February 1993, p. 70.

Table 26- shows how the family seeks to put controls on its members to prevent them from practising some acts that are considered deviant.

Area	Kamaliya					Fawwar				
Deeds	Yes	%	No	%	Total	Yes	%	No	%	Total
Drinking Alcohol	10	18.5	44	81.5	54	14	30	32	70	46
Sex work	51	95	3	5	54	43	93	3	7	46
Gambolling	23	42.5	31	57.5	54	16	35	30	65	46
Smoking	15	28	39	72	54	18	39	28	61	46
Wearing odd clothes	5	9	49	91	54	13	28	33	72	46

When reading the above table, we must note the following:

a. What is meant by controls here may start from guidance, warning, or reprimand and progress to prevention by using cruelty or any other means.

b. The word "sons" includes (boys and girls) and refers to juveniles and those under the age of maturity (18 years), and we tried to make a sample of households' heads understand that.

c. There must be many cautions related to the veracity of the information provided by the sample members of the research community, due to the sensitivity of the subject. That's because they are very reserved in front of a non-gypsy person who comes to them, and they assume that he is from the government, and came to take information about a case related to their violations or is looking for a lawbreaker. They also pretend to be unified with the wider (Iraqi) society in every way.

d. In most societies, there is a separation of the controls imposed on the girl from those imposed on the boy. There is no doubt that this separation exists in the gypsy community. But if it was put in the interview form, the results would be expected, which is claiming idealism and staying away from any suspicious thing that may harm their picture.

The role of the fieldwork study comes through the researcher's observation and participation in some situations and his interaction with the research community. In this regard, he noted the following:

1. Concerning drinking alcohol, if families set controls or prevent their sons from doing so, it is for economic reasons, not moral and ethical ones. We saw many children (males and females) drinking alcohol with their families or friends.

   Regarding sex work, there is a strong assertion that calls on the girl not to practice it, for reasons that we will explain later. Emphasizing that the girl retains her virginity before marriage is very important for most of the gypsies. The reasons are not related to honour for most of the gypsies, but rather to the importance of that in the first marriage for gypsies. It is a big deal, especially if the groom is not a gypsy, especially since it is sometimes done without a legal marriage contract in court. Or with a religious man (believer).

2. Regarding sex work, there is a strong assertion that calls on the girl not to practice it, for reasons that we will explain later. Emphasizing that the girl must retain her virginity before marriage is very important for most of gypsies. The reasons are not related to honour for most gypsies, but rather to its importance in the first marriage for gypsies, as it is a big deal, especially if the groom is not a gypsy, when it is sometimes done without a legal marriage contract in court or by a religious man (cleric).

3. As for gambling and smoking, if there is a ban and control over children, then the reasons are purely economic, represented in parents' fear of bearing their financial costs. We noticed that gambling sessions were conducted regularly, and they were sometimes allocated for important rich people from outside the gypsy community, and the gypsy girls or girls who lived with them participated in the game.

4. As for wearing odd or Western clothes, we observed wearing clothes that may not come to mind, especially among girls, such as (wearing very light and transparent clothes) or wearing a very short skirt (such as that of tennis players) and a bra (brassiere), while leaving the rest of the body exposed. Some wear clothes like the belly dance costumes that we saw in Arab films, or wear trousers and pants of different types and fashions.

Of course, wearing such clothes is understandable and is for temptation, as the girl goes out the door and stands in different positions, tempting men. That is different from the harassment we see in cities when men harass women.

When gypsies go to the cities, they are keen to wear clothes similar to the clothes of the society they go to. Some become conservative and they exaggerate their reservations. Some women wear the abaya (a traditional black cloth worn by women in conservative society), and some wear the Islamic abaya, especially when they go to the holy shrines for shopping or to go to the city's public bath. It is a kind of social adaptation to avoid harassment or remove any trace that may make others identify them.

Tribal organisations play a good role in controlling the behaviour of their members, and they also play other administrative and organisational roles. The strength of the tribal role depends on the weakness of the other roles of some sources of social control, such as the authority of law, and the extent of response and adaptation of this society and its submission to that authority.

The gypsy society is based by its nature on a tribal system. The head of the tribe, the tribal lineage, or the nomadic gypsy group is responsible for his group in front of the official or public authorities. His group members resort to him to resolve some disputes and quarrels as he has a moral impact on them. With the change like the gypsy community's life through stability, continuous civilized contact, their submission to the authority of law (the state), and changing their professions, the nature of the tribe influence and power also changed with it and became weak and depended on resolving some matters that are almost agreed upon, especially those that entail resorting to the police as they brought heavy consequences such as kidnapping, rape, and conflicts among members of the kinship unit.

Tribal sanctions:

There is no written (saniya) [146] among gypsies, like the rest of the Iraqi tribes. Conflicts and disputes among their members are resolved

---

[146] Saniyya is the local customary law written for each tribe or group of tribes, on which they agreed. In it, punishments and penalties are defined for each violation or crime committed, as well as solutions for problems and conflicts that occur within the tribe itself or one of its members against a person from another tribe.

by the sheikh, who is the chief of one of the most numerous tribes in the location of this gypsy group, which usually consists of households belonging to more than one tribe.

In the sheikh's council, where elders and notables of the gypsy community meet and impose their judgments in the case that the sheikh deals with. Their imposition (their decision) becomes valid, and its implementation is an inevitable duty.

The gypsies have many problems, whether among themselves or between them and the customers who visit their areas frequently. Problems that occur among the members of the gypsy community or with members of another gypsy group are usually resolved. And the judgments issued by the sheikh and the tribal or the gypsy group council are subject to personal estimates and current circumstances and are always affected by economic conditions.

Examples of sanctions are:
1. The blood money for the dead was until recently (15000-25000 dinars). Now it has reached (50,000 dinars, which is approximately equalled to 2500 US dollars). In case of intentional murder, the murderer is deported from one area to another. This amount of money is not agreed on but is subject to personal estimates.
2. The penalty for the crime of rape is that the perpetrator pays a double dowry to the girl, and the dowry is estimated by the members of the council and the sheikh. The amount reaches (100,000 dinars) or more. The perpetrator must also bear "al farsha" (which is the cost of food and drinks for the session of solving this problem).

3. If someone intentionally causes a permanent disability in another person, then the financial compensation amount for that equals half of the blood money.
4. As for the rest of the sanctions, they are determined during the sessions of the sheikh and the council of the gypsy community in the area. Flexibility can be noticed in penalties and sanctions that are imposed and are subject to the economic situation and the strength of the dinar, as they say, and according to the circumstances of the blockade.
5. The perpetrator or violator in most of these matters must also bear the costs of the problem-solving session. The kinship group participates in paying the costs dividing the amount equally according to their number (on heads) as they call it. Yet, the whole tribe is not obligated to do so as some refuse to pay or can't pay because of poverty or because they live in another area.
6. In some major and shameful crimes, such as murder and adultery, the perpetrator is the only one who is responsible for them.

Government authority began to appear in almost all aspects of their lives through the police forces, which almost continuously patrol the streets in Kamaliya area, due to the large number of problems that occur there, intermittently, or in need, as in Fawwar.

Al-Mukhtar now plays a major role, as he is the link between the state and the gypsies and began to replace the sheikh in many issues.

The data of the fieldwork study shows that the perception of the tribe and its role in social control became little and weaker in Kamaliya area where 90% of the study sample did not pay attention to it, while it was 72% in Fawwar. This is undoubtedly the result of the role dispensing of the tribe and the weakness of kinship relations.

The data of the study shows that only 14% of Kamaliya participated in the payment of blood money with the tribe, but this percentage rose to 19% in Fawwar.

As these tribal obligations are a kind of social solidarity. They are a heavy burden on the family and encourage committing crimes or offences. The individual feels reassured in advance that there is someone who eases the burden and bears and shares the consequences with him. They also diminish the role of law and official authority.

Social control conclusion:
1. The gypsies are generally affected by the general means of social control of the Iraqi society, through their adaptation to some of them, even partially, and their attempt to apply them in their official dealings or with the public.
2. The gypsies, in the eyes of others, are outside public control (law, mores and religion), and thus they form a culture that contracts with it and therefore, they are exposed to social exclusion or prejudice.
3. The most important factor of social control among the gypsies is the rule of law (the police), which is a major deterrent to them and comes first, then comes the role of religion and then mores through tribal obligations. Finally, comes the factors of the public opinion, the sense of belonging to the gypsy community, which binds it most and preserves its structure, the factor of unification within the framework of the gypsy community, the sense of united destiny due to the outside threat, social rejection, and prejudice against them from outside the gypsy community.

4. There are no strict control factors on children in terms of alcohol consumption, gambling, and smoking, and if they are available, they are for purely financial purposes aimed at saving money and not letting children share them with their parents.

5. The gypsy area in Fawwar is characterized by being more compatible with the factors of social control than the gypsy area in Kamaliya, and thus it is closer in adaptation to the wider community.

Chapter Eight

Communication & interaction

Communication

Social interaction

Models of social interaction between the gypsies and their
social environment

Communication & interaction conclusion

Communication:

Communication is a social process during which ideas and information are transferred and exchanged directly or indirectly between two or more parties within a social system by using communication means that rely on written, visual, or audio words and symbols, with the intent of informing, knowing, persuading, influencing, or suggesting certain ideas and orientations, provided the occurrence of responses, certain reactions or reactions to the stimulus or communication message. [147]

Communication is the process, situation, or tool by which the components of culture are transferred from a source called the sender to another called the receiver. This transmission process takes place through one channel or several communication channels, and the most important communication channels are:

Language:
Gestures and body movement.

Arts:
Radio
Television
Newspaper and magazines
Flyers, posters, and printed advertising.

---

[147] Arif, Majeed, The Anthropology of Communication, Dar Al-Hikma, Baghdad, 1990, p. 14.

It is possible to add modern means of communication related to the Internet, such as e-mail, Messenger, Paltalk, websites, and other electronic media.

The forms of civilized communication differ according to the foundations on which it is based in studying it. These forms include: [148] direct and indirect communication, war and peace communication, and primary and secondary communication.

As for social interaction, it is the mutual influence between the behaviour of individuals and groups through the process of communication and interaction. It also means what results from human nature in terms of mutual influence between the social and cultural forces themselves, which is the product of social interaction. [149] The contact that occurs between the gypsy community as a sub-culture and the Iraqi society as a totalitarian society (dominant culture) is direct and continuous. Social interaction caused a change in many of the gypsy's lifestyles and led to rapprochement and adaptation in many aspects of social life.

"And the reality of communication is the transmission, disclosure, or exchange of ideas, opinions, or information by speech, writing, or signs that communicate or transmit a document, message, mobile views, or materials.[150]

The gypsies were given opportunities to communicate, in varying degrees, through all channels of communication. The direct contact

---

[148] Arif, ibid., p. 152.
[149] Sugarman, Barry, Op. Cit, p. 214.
[150] New Webster dictionary, P. 321.

is complete and continuous between the gypsies and the Iraqi society, through daily dealings and interaction through the gypsies' professions. These professions require dealing with non-gypsies, as we saw in the economic pattern, as well as through their frequent visits to the markets and official departments of the state. This led to the formation of friendship or neighbouring and economic relations (buyer, seller, and mediator). If most of these relationships are of interest (exchange of benefit according to the theory of social exchange that we referred to, and we will refer to that more in social adaptation). [151] This means the participation of all systems of social construction in the process of communication and civilizational spread. Therefore, the change will extend to dominate these systems or members. This is what we aim for, as this means that change will be directed towards adapting as much as possible to the broader society or some of its civilized features.

Cultural communication does its job in bringing about cultural changes that affect (acculturated) societies because of (cultural communication). This change may extend to one of the social structures of one of the parties interacting in this process. Disintegration and decay affect one of its existing social systems, such as the penetration and spread of certain religions in one of the societies, which causes many changes in most cities and social institutions.

Irving Hallowell, the anthropologist, referred to that and the importance of communication and influence saying: "In recent years, scientists have shown an increasing interest in studying the mutual influence

---

[151] Palmor, Hirsch & Ariffin, International Communication and the Diffusion of Family Planning in West Malaysia- Demography Publication of the Population on Association of America, vol. 8, No. 3, August 1971, p. 413.

among different cultures to the extent that this topic has become at the top of cultural anthropological research". [152]

The influence can be mutual between the gypsies as a sub-culture and the wider society. [153] We have seen the influence of gypsies on the prevailing culture. As for its influence on society, there is no doubt that their presence and the work they practice are a constant attraction factor for a large segment of young people (who visit them frequently as customers or immigrants of both sexes), although the influence on young females is less than that of males, due to the nature of our conservative society.

Civilized communication has important results, which are classified into four types: [154]

1- Fusion 2- Retention 3- Resistance and Separation 4- Conflict and Revolutions.

These results are subject to the conditions experienced by the cultured groups that are exposed to civilized contact.

Models of social interaction between the gypsies and their social environment:
Since the gypsies of Kamaliya live in an open area and relate to

[152] Linton, Ralph, Anthropology, and the Crisis of the Modern World, translated by Abd al-Malik al-Nashif, the Modern Library, Beirut, 1967, p. 300.
[153] Al-Samarrai, Mutaib and Al-Hashimi, Hamied, The Impact of Mid-state Characteristics on Social Behaviour, a paper presented at the first conference of the Faculty of Arts, Qadisiya University, 1994, unpublished.
[154] Arif, The Anthropology of Communication, Op. Cit, p159.

residential areas of non-gypsies. And because Kamaliya area lies within the capital, Baghdad, there is continuous and direct contact and interaction between the gypsies and non-gypsies according to mutual interests.

As for Fawwar area, as a model for the rest of the areas inhabited by the gypsies, it lies at a distance of approximately (12 km from the nearest city) (Diwaniyah) and it is an isolated village for the gypsies. The nearest village bordering it is the village of Al Jamiyya, 2 km away, where some shops meet some of the people's needs. The presence of the shops there shrank the gypsies' visits to the city and their contact with it or with the neighbouring villages compared to the Kamaliya area. However, the data from the interview form shows that (57%) of the research sample families indicate their continuous visits to the city for shopping. We see that the reasons for this are the very high prices in the gypsy area compared to city prices, even though transportation costs are high between the area and Diwaniyah or other nearby cities. There is no doubt that the calculation of the financial difference is what drives them to do so, just as the village shops do not meet their needs.

Table -27 shows the fields that some family members enrolled in.

Area	Kamaliya			Fawwar		
	Male	Female	Total	Male	Female	Total
Driving course	10	-	10	3	-	3
Music course	3	-	3	2	-	2
Dancing course	-	3	3	-	2	2
Musical band	7	8	15	-	-	-
Association /union	5	5	10	3	3	6
Total	25	16	41	8	6	14

Enrolling in such courses and participation in work with non-gypsies is a great indicator of communication and interaction between the gypsies and Iraqi society.

The above data showed that the number of male participants or those who enrolled in the courses mentioned above is higher than that of the females. However, the number of female participants in dance courses or those who enrolled in artistic teams is higher than that of males. The data also showed that none of the research sample's female members enrolled in a driving course or a music learning course.

The number of members in artistic bands, an association, or a syndicate is rising for both sexes, even if it is less than it should or is expected, especially since singing is one of their main professions, and it must be developed and directed, whether by them or the state's guidance. What increases the number of artistic members is getting a work permit to work in nightclubs and places that require it.

From the comparison between the two study areas, it is noted that communication opportunity is more available for Kamaliya gypsies because of its location in Baghdad, the capital, unlike Fawwar gypsies in Diwaniyah.

Table - 28 - shows the workplace for makeup, grooming and hairdressing for the girls in the sample.

Place	House	Area	City	Total
Kamaliya	15	30	9	54
%	28	55	17	100
Fawwar	20	-	26	46
%	43	-	57	100

Gypsy girls visit hairdressers in cities frequently and constantly, which means continuous contact and interaction, on a (benefit exchange) basis, of course, but it also undoubtedly means a process of civilized transference through communication, learning and using civilized methods of grooming and hairdressing, in addition to the mutual influence in behaviour through simulation and imitation.

In this regard, Comparing the two areas of the study appears that Fawwar gypsy women's frequent visits to hairdressers in the nearby cities (Diwaniyah and Afak) are more than that of Kamaliya gypsy women, although less than half of the sample do their grooming at home, and we believe that it is due to the following:
1. Fawwar gypsy area does not have a women's hairdressing salon.
2. There are many women's hairdressing salons in the Kamaliya area, close to the gypsies' homes.
3. Home grooming, when women do make up for themselves, is higher in Fawwar than it is in Kamaliya.

It's worth mentioning here, concerning direct communication, that the gypsy women frequently visit the city's public bath, and this is very much common in Fawwar (see the economic chapter).

Table 29- Preferred patient therapy location.

Location	Home	Area	City	Total
Kamaliya	31	20	3	54
%	57	47	6	100
Fawwar	25	15	6	46
%	54	33	13	100

Places like hospitals and clinics are important places that can play an important role in the process of communication and interaction among different ethnic groups. Visiting these places frequently makes them feel a sense of flexibility and tolerance. It is the consequences of being subject to one criterion that builds on one criterion and makes them feel similar. Before all that, it indicates the submission of this group to the logic and reality of modern science. referring to its adaptation to it, as this group broke their shell, known as traditional medicine, replacing it with modern medicine.

Depending on that, it is possible to measure this aspect of communication among the gypsies. We found that the percentage is almost close in both study areas (Kamaliya and Fawwar), although the percentage of those who prefer traditional medicine in Fawwar area is higher than it is in Kamaliya. We believe that the best explanation for this is that most of them suffer from diseases that cannot be treated in doctors' clinics and hospitals, such as (impotence and psychological and mental diseases). They believe that the reasons behind those diseases are a sort of magic (beads: when a woman did magic – which is put in food – to a man to force him or prevent him from marrying another woman, or to incapacitate him sexually). They believe that the remedy for this magic is also through another magic or by resorting to holy shrines.

Lots of gypsies go to see doctors in clinics and the reason behind that, as some informants told the researcher, is that most of those patients suffer from venereal diseases (gonorrhoea, syphilis, and possibly HIV). [155]

The reason why patients with this type of disease come to clinics and not to hospitals is the desire not to reveal this matter to government agencies because these diseases are usually caused by illegal sexual intercourse. Also, the sex trade is a major profession for them, and they generally fear the consequences of that.

Table 30- shows whether the studied households have literate members who read newspapers.

Area	Yes	No	Total
Kamaliya	16	38	54
%	30	70	100
Fawwar	8	38	46
%	17	83	100

---

[155] I did not get a firm confirmation or denial of the existence of AIDS, when I met the responsible authorities, including Dr Hassan Alwan, health prevention officer at Al-Tali'ah Hospital in Diwaniyah, which is responsible for such cases and for sending health teams to villages, including the gypsy village of Fawwar. Dr Alwan told me that HIV test samples are sent to the ministry and kept secret, as no official announcement has been made of AIDS cases in Iraq so far.

Different media types (read, heard, or seen) have a major role in communicating the vocabulary of culture. They even have a great influence on directing individuals' character, life and style, whether they are aware of that or not. Its impact depends on the quality of what it presents, the recipient's level of education, and the extent of its communication with him/her. Newspapers and magazines have an important role in this aspect. Reading newspapers by the gypsy family, for example, means that they are asking for more culture and would like to see what is going on in the country and the world. This means the ability to learn and interact with the country and the world, and the possibility of being influenced by it. It means mind flexibility to accept what is sent to it, as well as the feeling of removing the psychological and material barriers between him/her and others, as well as between him/her and the members of society. It also means the possibility of positively influencing his family and relatives. And through newspapers and magazines, girls can follow fashion. As for the study sample of Kamaliya and Fawwar gypsy areas, the data of the interview questionnaire showed that the number of literate members of the gypsy households in Kamaliya is higher than it in Fawwar, and the reasons for that are:

1. The number of educated people in Kamaliya is higher than it is in Fawwar.
2. Kamaliya lies in Baghdad, the capital, and this firstly means that newspapers are available and secondly, the gypsies there are somewhat affected by the cultural atmosphere.

As for television, which is said to be the most dangerous media device because it is in direct contact with the family and affects the young and the old positively and negatively without exception. All gypsies in Kamaliya have TV sets and few of them in Fawwar don't. On the contrary, the number of gypsies who have radio and tape player devices in Fawwar is higher than it is in Kamaliya, perhaps to cover the lack of TV sets there.

As for the owners of video player sets, their number is higher in Kamaliya, because of the high economic and social level.

Kamaliya area is distinguished from the rest of the gypsy communities in Iraq by having telephone lines, due to their location within Baghdad, the capital, unlike the rest of the areas that do not fall even within the borders of the municipalities of nearby cities. Cars play an important role as a direct transportation means, and the taxi driver has a large share of contact with different types of disparate human behaviour, and through that, he gains great flexibility in dealing with and is affected by many of them. Cars are also a means that helps speed up communication by shortening distance and time.

Conclusion of communication and social interaction:
1. The gypsies have great opportunities for civilized contact with the broader Iraqi society and its various channels.
2. The gypsies in the Kamaliya area are more fortunate than their counterparts in Fawwar in terms of communication and social interaction because Kamaliya lies in Baghdad. It is an open area and exposed to various types of daily communication and interaction, besides having great services that contribute to interaction and adaptation with the wider community.
3. The interpretation of social exchange theory, presented by Homans, says: "It is an exchange of benefits and services, through which each actor tries to reduce costs and maximize profits". Homans

calls this direct interaction among individuals a (primary social behaviour).

4. The research hypothesis that says: (The process of social interaction leads to a kind of adaptation) was achieved through studying and analysing the social interaction among the members of the gypsy community and the Iraqi community.

Chapter Nine

Social Adaptation:

Entrance

Models of social adaptation

Social acceptance

Gypsies' view of their reality

Conclusion

Social Adaptation

We study social adaptation here as being all individual or collective (human) processes or attempts that seek to adapt to the prevailing natural and cultural environment, or those similar processes intended from outside towards the individual or group to achieve the same purpose. These processes may lead to complete or semi-complete integration with the prevailing cultural, social or natural environment.

Sub Committee of the Social Research Council stated that cultural adaptation refers to the phenomena that result from the direct and continuous contact between two cultures, and the consequent changes in the patterns of the original culture. This is what we will focus on in our study of the gypsies' cultural and social adaptation as a sub-culture within Iraqi society.

The analysis of cultural changes follows the following approach:

It starts with descriptive abstractions of the stable cultural forms to go through a series of processes related to the conditions that prompted individuals to adjust their ways of adaptation. And then returns to the effects of adjusted adaptation and its repercussions on social conditions, describing them as new or adjusted cultural forms. Thus, it can be said that the problems of cultural change are related to the situations and processes that lead to an adaptive adjustment in the individual behaviour that has acquired a special social significance. [156]

---

[156] Linton, Ralph, Op. Cit, pp. 309-310.

None of these factors or roles fully applies to the processes of change that the gypsies experience. They cover most of them, such as replacement and addition, for many aspects, systems, and institutions.

These change processes were characterized by conciliation, as old features merged with new ones, whereas cultural disintegration occurs in most social systems.

As for the form changes, they were the unification and assimilation of many cultural features and the integration of some other features. The gypsy community did not reach full integration with the Iraqi society, yet, it did not extinct either, like what happened to some ethnic groups in North and South America.

Adaptation is characterized by selectivity and uniqueness, as they select traits and adapt to them, and are unique from others in their cultural ways.

We focused on models or manifestations of social adaptation that deserve mention and research, they are:

1. Religion (We did not discuss religion here in detail because we discussed it in a separate chapter in the study)
2. Stability
3. Language
4. Fashion as changes or appearance adaptation.
5. Friendship
6. Intermarriage (intermarriage with non-gypsies)
7. Neighborhood

8. National affiliation, as a fundamental and most sensitive change, which indicates social acceptance.

Models of the gypsies' social adaptation with their social surroundings:

First: Nationalism (a sense of affiliation to the big community).

The nationality document is the most important thing that helps a person or a group to adapt and integrate into the larger society. Without it, the individual loses confidence in his/her future and faces many difficulties that stand against his/her right, as a human being, to have a normal life. Thus, its absence reduces his/her giving and achievement and his/her keenness for the public interest and increases his/her own or his/her group's isolation and the prejudice of the prevailing culture (wider society) against the group.

The problem of the national ID was one of the most important problems that the gypsies in Iraq suffered from until the beginning of the eighties when they were treated as foreigners because they were not granted the Iraqi nationality ID.

Decisions were issued in 1924, 1959 and 1962 concerning gypsies. Resolution 24, issued in 1924, did not consider them as foreigners. Resolution 16390 of 1959 declared them stateless aliens while Resolution 6 issued in 1962 agreed to grant them citizenship with conditions. [157]

---

[157] The Directorate of Nationality Affairs, Qadisiya Governorate Branch, a pamphlet that includes a summary about the gypsy, and it is internally circulated.

Ministerial Order no. 14167 of 1-8-1964 required the formation of a committee for this purpose, and approved granting them on the following conditions:

1. He/she must be registered as a gypsy in one of the public population records.
2. He/she should be able to speak Arabic.
3. He/she must not be a nomad.
4. He/she must have a known profession.
5. He/she must not be affiliated with a foreign country.

However, the committee failed due to the presence of a previous telegram from the Ministry of Interior confirming that they are nomads and cannot be granted Iraqi citizenship.

In 1974, a circular was issued by the Directorate of General Civil Status confirming the freezing of registered gypsies' records. [158]

As a result, the gypsies suffered from several problems, perhaps the most important of which are:

1. Ownership problem, as restrictions are imposed on foreigners concerning owning property.
2. Job and employment problems.
3. Services and education problems.

The refusal to grant citizenship and the consequent material and psychological damage undoubtedly leads to the gypsies' alienation and lack of adaptation and harmony with Iraqi society on the one

---

[158] Al-Hadithi, Taha Hammadi, Gypsies and Qarach in Iraq, University of Mosul, 1979, pp. 157-158.

hand and distorts the attitude of Iraqi society towards them on the other.

This certainly results in a weak sense of affiliation and feeling towards the wider community, and that is one of the most important obstacles to social adaptation.

Table 31- shows the extent of the gypsies' sense of affiliation to the wider community.

Area	Yes	No	Total
Kamaliya	54	-	54
%	100	-	100
Fawwar	46	-	46
%	100	-	100

The above table shows that all sample members in both study areas feel that they belong to the larger community, which means an important step towards social integration and adaptation.

Second: Stability:
Stability is a great asset for every nomadic community or group. Nomadism was the most important characteristic of the gypsies, so that they are described as nomadic in many countries of the world because of the nature of their life. [159]

Instability is one of the common features of the gypsies in the world, including the gypsies of Iraq. We believe that the following are the reasons behind nomadism: doing professions which are despised in

---

[159] See Greenfield, Howard, Gypsies, Crown Publishers, Inc., New York, 1977.

the eyes of most of the peoples they pass through. This characteristic of nomadism made them abuse and wreak havoc in their path, which causes harm to the societies they pass through. This is a characteristic of most of the passers-by (renegades), which is a lack of sense of responsibility, because they believe that they do not bear the consequences of their deeds as they cannot be convicted, due to their rapid movement and elusiveness.

Among the crimes they were accused of (theft, kidnapping - kidnapping women and children -, witchcraft and sorcery and even cannibalism. [160]

Some of the gypsies of the world are proud of this nomadic characteristic and they justify it as a symbol of freedom and lack of submission to authority. The gypsy looks at the rest of the non-gypsy people with a look of contempt and calls others (Gadjo), which means a farmer or devious, and it is intended to mean complete humiliation and degradation, just as the meaning of (rude) or (impolite) or (serf). Yet, the gypsies consider themselves the masters of the land. [161]

We heard and observed the gypsies using the word (Gadjo), pronounced as (Kadji) to refer to the non-gypsies and sometimes they called them (Arabs) too.

Third: Language:
Learning and using the language of the wider society (dominant culture) by the minority group (subculture) are the most important

[160] Greenfield, Op. Cit, 11.
[161] Clebert, Jean-Paul, The Gypsies: A Folkloric Historical Study, translated by Lutfi Al-Khoury, Cultural Affairs House, Baghdad, 1976, p. 9.

tools of social adaptation. Language is a means of understanding, rapprochement, and knowing the laws, values, and customs of the wider society. Learning shortens the path to social adaptation. As mentioned earlier, the gypsies are quick to adapt, especially in the fields of language, fashion and religion.

Thus, the gypsies appear in every country speaking the language of that country, although they have an original language. The wide distances that separate them in the world, and the nature of their living styles, made some regional groups maintain a special language that is a mixture of several languages. As a result of their travel and continuous mixing with different peoples.

The International Journal of the Sociology of Language devoted a special issue to research the languages and dialects of the gypsy groups in Europe and America.

In Iraq, the gypsies were able to assimilate the Arabic language fully and accurately with an accent which is close to the Bedouin accent.

Most of the gypsies almost forget their original language, and even their young children do not fully know their language except for a few words.

This is due to several reasons, including:
1. There is no written alphabet for them.
2. Illiteracy prevails in the gypsy communities.
3. They were dispersed and separated into small groups in most of the late centuries.

4. They move continuously which leads to instability and mixing with many societies, which means that they acquire new vocabulary and then gradually abandon their original language.

The gypsies in Iraq now use vocabulary from their original language, which is a mixture of several languages (Persian, Arabic, Kurdish and Turkish). They use vocabulary, including passwords or riddles when needed, especially in the presence of a stranger (Kadji) who is not a gypsy.

For example, if someone wanted to inform his family or the people of his area about the arrival of the police, he would say to them: (Amd Rusti ha), which means (the police came), or (Rusti, Rusti), which means (police, police).

What is the parents' position when they see that their children do not know their native language?

They feel disappointed most of the time and embarrassed more often. A situation like this occurred in our presence during the fieldwork study, when the head of the family said to his son (Jib Kawi), meaning (bring the carcass), and the son did not understand what the father wanted.

In this regard, the following question showed the results below:

Table -32-: Are you keen to teach your son or daughter your native language?

Area	Yes	No	Total
Kamaliya	7	47	54
%	13	87	100
Fawwar	10	36	46
%	12	88	100

The motive of (ethnicity or group pride) does not exist, in its precise meaning here, in the gypsy individual, rather the gypsy individual feels inferior towards other non-gypsies.

Finally, we say that the use of the dominant language of society by the gypsies (as a minority group) is one of the most important aspects of social adaptation.

Table -33-: Some words from the gypsy language and their meaning in English.

Gypsy word	Meaning	Gypsy word	Meaning
Khardin خاردين	food	Rasti	Police-government
Bazar بازار	market	Tabala طبالة	Officer
Khuda خدا	God	Aw آو	Water
Serma سرما	rain	Tiniyat تينيات	Chickens
Aluhi الوهي	sun	Kawi كاوي	Carcass
Jeeb جيب	bring	Jomin ha ها جومن	Clothes
Kadgi كجي	A stranger (non-gypsy)	Joqa جوقا	Abaya
Besrak بسراك	A boy	desmala دسمالة	Men head cover
Dentrak دنتراك	A boy	Bendko بندكو	Mens headband
Bemarda بيماردة	A woman	Kwesh كويش	A shoe
Amid آمد	Came	Kara ها كار	Stuff
Kiyaha كياها	Old	Nun نون	Bread

Fourth: Fashion:

The gypsies have been distinguished by their rapid adaptation, especially in material appearances, to the peoples whom they live within, including fashion as they wear the costumes of those peoples, especially those who have a great deal of sensitivity towards the gypsies' various professions except for some countries in which they were known for their distinctive costumes. [162]

Wearing the costumes of the prevailing culture by the sub-culture is undoubtedly an ingenious adaptive aspect that achieves a kind of social symmetry with others, albeit in appearance. The gypsies used this method to arouse the sympathy of the wider society within which they live on the one hand and to avoid suspicion so that they would not be distinguished on the other hand, because most groups and people warn of them, due to what is known about their undesirable actions.

The gypsies in Iraq wear the same customs as the Iraqi society. Men's fashion includes the Arab dress (dishdasha, sayah, or about) , a shemagh or keffiyeh with a headband on it, leather shoes or leather slippers, and the men's abaya. It is like the Bedouin or rural dress.

Youth fashion includes trousers and shirts in general, especially when they go to cities and markets The rest of the time they wear dishdashas with long pants underneath. As for women's clothing, it includes the women's dress with an abaya over it when they go to the city. Girls wear modern clothes (skirts and shirts or modern women's dresses),

---

[162] Prof. Dr Majeed Aref told the author that the gypsies in Bulgaria and Finland are distinguished by their embroidered costumes, which are distinguished from the rest of the people of those countries.

and they wear regular or Islamic abayas. Moreover, some girls wear women's pants (trousers) or short clothes, which add attractiveness and temptation, and this happens especially in times of work or parties (see the economic system chapter).

Table -34- shows how gypsies are keen to wear others' costumes in other cities and villages.

Area	Yes	No	Total
Kamaliya	28	26	54
%	52	48	100
Fawwar	35	11	46
%	76	24	100

The above data shows that those who are keen to wear clothes like the clothes of the community close to them in Fawwar area are more than their counterparts in Kamaliya. That is due to the keenness of the gypsies of Fawwar to avoid the problems of sexual harassment, especially with their women in particular. That is added to the harassment that they may face if they do not adhere to the fashion of the society close to them, especially if known as gypsies (as their shapes and physical characteristics easily distinguish them from others). (See chapter the Gypsies' Characteristics chapter).

Most Kamaliya gypsies do not adhere to wearing a certain costume or are more conservative because they live in one of Baghdad's suburbs. It is known that the capital, Baghdad, includes a mixture of cultures, a variety of costumes, and great anonymity. This means that there are no problems like those the gypsies of Fawwar may face in Qadisiya Governorate, and therefore this can apply to other similar gypsy areas in Iraq.

A result:

Gypsies' wearing costumes like those of the society in which they live is a necessary condition to avoid problems that they may face if they violate that, and this represents another aspect of the gypsies' social adaptation.

Fifth: Social Acceptance:

Social acceptance is an important indicator of social adaptation, and it is a sign of satisfaction for both transaction parties. Engaging in joint business, dealing, friendship, marriage, and neighbourhood are the most important indicators of social acceptance. We can say that these matters are fundamental changes and not just superficial, and they are matters that do not accept courtesy. Marriage means merging, living under one roof, bearing common responsibilities, revealing all secrets, exchanging emotions, and having children because of this social process. Friendship, on its part, means the abolition of class, sectarian, and racial differences, as it represents mental and emotional rapprochement.

As far as neighbourly relations are concerned, they indicate acceptance through interaction, close living, and tolerance. In Arab traditions, it is said (the neighbour before the house). This indicates the importance of the neighbourly relationship, as the neighbour can greatly affect his/her neighbour negatively or positively.

Engaging in joint business with the gypsies, such as investing capital, partnering in stores, working together, buying, and selling transactions, etc., are of great importance in reflecting the extent of social acceptance and satisfaction.

It is worth pointing out first that the gypsies do not engage in joint business with others unless they feasibly study it, and make sure that its results are guaranteed for their benefit, and thus the exchange theory applies to them.

Table 35- shows how much the gypsy study sample members prefer to join non-gypsies in shared business, a comparison between the two study areas.

Area	Yes	No	Total
Kamaliya	20	34	54
%	37	63	100
Fawwar	7	39	54
%	15	85	100

From the previous table, the percentage appears higher in Kamaliya than in Fawwar for those who prefer to engage in joint work with non-gypsies in the first area, due to its openness to Baghdad, unlike the second area. It also provides the requirements for the work that they will enter. For example, if they enter the field of music, there is a huge number of artists (singers, musicians and female and male dancers), song and party recording companies. However, the availability of venues for parties such as nightclubs, theatres, and artistic groups (see the economic system chapter).

Commercial businesses have more opportunities to succeed in Kamaliya than in Fawwar. It is more possible for non-gypsy people to enter Kamaliya without reservation, due to the great anonymity there, and because of the capacity and diversity of Baghdadi society, unlike the region of Qadisiya governorate. Engaging joint business with the gypsies is considered a stigma because the community there is conservative as they carry prejudice against the gypsies and their scientific, skilful and experiential incompetence compared to others.

It is clear to the researcher and worth mentioning that the gypsies, in general, are afraid of non-gypsies, especially if they go outside their areas because they do not trust non-gypsies because of the community's ostracism against them. They fear the revenge of someone who was beaten, quarrelled or defrauded in their areas whom they may meet outside their area. It is known that they are often exposed to such incidents.

In the gypsy areas, as was mentioned in the economic system chapter, many problems occur constantly with customers (al keyafah) because of several issues, the most important of which are:
1. Their work's nature, such as singing, drinking alcohol, and the sex trade, creates problems and quarrels.
2. Recklessness of both parties, since the gypsies are illiterate and their feeling of being deviated from religion, law and general custom create those problems. In addition, most of the gypsies' visitors are reckless young, and they despise gypsies and that often provokes the latter.
3. The absence of police supervision, especially in isolated gypsy areas, including Fawwar.

Table -36- shows how much the family suffers from problems with some people in the cities and neighbouring areas (a comparison between the two study areas).

Area	Yes	No	Total
Kamaliya	5	49	54
%	9	91	100
Fawwar	25	21	46
%	54	46	100

The results above, by comparing the two study areas, show that the gypsies of Fawwar suffer more when they come to cities close to them, because they are easily distinguished from others, and because the urban communities are limited and conservative.

Table -37- shows some of the problems that gypsies face when they come to cities.

Problems / Area	Harassment	Despising	Financial exploitation	Other	Total
Kamaliya	2	2	1	-	5
%	40	40	20	-	100
Fawwar	12	8	5	-	25
%	48	32	20	-	100

The above table, which completes the previous one, shows that the difference between the two study areas is that the Fawwar area has the highest level of problems with others that gypsies face. It is noted that the percentage of harassment problems by others is high. The reason for that is the ideas and perceptions that non-gypsies have of gypsies. This image is also reflected in the problem of despising them and calling them insulting phrases.

Sixth: Friendship:
It is one of the positive relationships that bind two or more persons based on intellectual, ethnic, religious, professional, or regional affinity. Tonnies believes that friendship is independent of kinship and neighbourhood, and it stems from the sensational sharing that may occur because of similarity in work and thinking tendencies. Misha Titieve believes that friendship plays a role in the cohesion of society members who are not bound by kinship ties.[163]

In Arab heritage, it was said (A friend in need is a friend indeed), (One friend, not a thousand enemies), and (May someone be a brother of yours that your mother never gave birth to), referring to the friend. All of these and others confirm the importance of friend and friendship as a human relationship that can play the role of kinship or more.

Friendship is an important indicator of social acceptance and even paves the way to cultural representation.[164]

Our study of friendship in this research comes for the purpose of finding out the degree of acceptance and adaptation reached by the gypsies in Iraq and finding out the nature of this relationship, if any.

Table 38 shows whether gypsies have non-gypsy friends or not.

Area	Yes	No	Total
Kamaliya	37	17	54
%	68	32	100
Fawwar	30	16	46
%	65	35	100

Al-Fuja'a House, Qatar, 1986, pp. 168-169.
[164] Ibid, p168.

The data of the above table shows that the percentage of those who have friends from outside their gypsy community from the two study areas is higher in Kamaliya than it in Fawwar.

We believe that the reasons for that are related primarily to the non-gypsy people, due to their perception of the gypsies and the nature of their interaction with them. The attitude towards dealing with gypsies is more conservative in the provinces than it is in Baghdad.

We shouldn't forget that these relations are mutually beneficial, that is, built based on the mutual interest of the parties. This is shown by the fact that they are temporary depending on circumstances and the interests that control them.

Table 39 shows whether friendship relations with non-gypsies are temporary or continuous.

Area	Yes	No	Total
Kamaliya	31	6	37
%	83	17	100
Fawwar	25	5	30
%	83	17	100

The data of the previous table shows that most relationships are temporary in both study areas. This means that they are based on temporary interest, and that this relationship depends on the circumstance that governs it. Therefore, when you ask the gypsies, "who are your friends?" They answer that (they are police officers, sheikhs, businessmen, or notables, mentioning them by names).

This indicates the inefficiency of this relationship, and they call this a friendship relationship, even though they know that it is not permanent if it really exists. They claimed these relationships to give themselves importance and to complement those notables. Gypsies are in constant need to solve their multiple problems.

There are other friendships built based on mutual benefit with pleasure and mirth seekers, especially rich ones. They privately prepare mirth sessions and women for them, usually at night, either in the gypsies' houses or those people's own homes (such as orchards and villas). In some gypsies' houses, you can find certain girl is dedicated to a certain person (who is known by others) and not to someone else and she cannot be given to anybody other than him. These deals are done for huge amounts of money agreed on by those gypsies' (friends).

As proof that these relations are not equal, mutual visits do not take place, and it is likely that the parents of these gypsy friends are not always aware of or satisfied with this friendship, as we were informed by some of the non-gypsy informants. The following table shows whether there are visits between the gypsies and their friends and if the gypsies visit their non-gypsy friends at home. The following table shows that.

Table – 40- shows where the gypsy meets his non-gypsy friend in case the visit happens.

Place / Area	House	Shop	Public place	Other	Total
Kamaliya	2	7	4	1	14
%	14	51	28	7	100
Fawwar	1	6	2	1	10
%	10	60	20	10	100

As mentioned above, these percentages show the weakness of these relationships and the foundation on which they are built.

Result:

Friendship relations between the gypsy and non-gypsy individuals are material-interest relations, and social exchange theory can be applied to them based on self-interest and the amount of profit obtained.

Seventh: Affinity:

Affinity is a social relationship among individuals and groups linked by marriage. The affinity and descent bonds may come together in the in-laws, when the husband and wife are related by descent relations, they were from the same family (cousins) or from the same family lineage. [165]

Affinity is a strong social relationship that imposes varying obligations on its members, depending on their degree of closeness and type of connection.

What we are interested in here is the relationship between the gypsies on the one hand and other Iraqis on the other.

This type of marriage is the so-called mixed family (a small group consisting of a husband and wife, differing in their ethnological, cultural, national, religious, and even ethnic background, and the

---

[165] Mair, Lucy, Op. Cit, P.424.

children of the family share the ethnological and national features of one of the parents and ignoring the other). [166]

What makes us call this such intermarriage (between gypsies and other Iraqis) is the consensus on the unwillingness to establish such relationships with gypsies. This means that there are significant barriers separating the gypsy community from the wider society, which are primarily their professional characteristics and then their culture.

Marriage is considered the most important indicator of social acceptance degree among ethnic groups. The cases of intermarriage were the marriage of an Arab man (non-gypsy) to a gypsy girl. These marriages are completely rejected by the husband's parents, and these marriages are not carried out in the common customary way in Iraqi society.

Table 41 shows the number of times in which gypsy men marry non-gypsy women.

Area	Yes	No	Total
Kamaliya	4	50	54
%	7	93	100
Fawwar	3	43	46
%	6	94	100

The data above shows that the number of gypsy men who married non-gypsy women is small due to the following:

---

[166] Al Hassan, Problems of Inter-Marriage and Mixed Families, Al-Taliya House, Beirut, 1994, p24.

1. No one of non-gypsy man accepts to marry his daughter to a gypsy man.
2. Most of the women who can marry gypsy men are those who come to the gypsy areas frequently or whose circumstances have thrown them into (sex work): (see the economic pattern chapter, sex trade). That is why young gypsies do not prefer to marry them because they are (sex workers).

Marriages of gypsy men to non-gypsy women either happened when those men picked them up before they indulged in sin, or some of them accepted to marry those women as they were, even if they were sex workers because dowries for the gypsy women were expensive.

The study showed that in all such marriages, the wife resides with the husband in his region.

Table - 42-shows the number of marriages of a non-gypsy man to a gypsy girl according to the study sample and a comparison between the two studied areas.

Area	Yes	No	Total
Kamaliya	10	44	54
%	19.5	80.5	100
Fawwar	9	37	46
%	20.5	79.5	100

There were considerable affinity cases, as shown in the table above, and at a similar rate in the two areas.

These marriages are characterized by the following:
1. These marriages are conducted as part of large deals of money.

Gypsies are keen to marry off their daughters as a first marriage for a large sum of money since the amounts of some dowries (bride price) reached one hundred or one hundred and fifty thousand dinars (approximately four to six thousand dollars). This is undoubtedly a very large amount for the average Iraqi citizen under the circumstances of the blockade, that is why girls are married off to rich men.

2. These marriages are temporary, as their purpose is to satisfy the sexual desire and whim of love and admiration of these admiring men. The marriage takes place in exchange for a large amount of money, then the wife returns to her family after a short period, which may be weeks or days.

3. Most of these marriages are illegitimate or illegal, as they are not registered in courts or by a cleric.

4. Most of these marriages do not form real families, because of their nature or the basis on which they are built. Children are often victims of such marriages, as some children or their families do not even know the names of their fathers. We found a girl in Al Islah school in Fawwar area. Her father wasn't known for sure to be an Egyptian or a Sudanese, and she was completely ignorant of even his name, and her family registered her in the name of her grandfather (of her mother's side). Similarly, there are also many of her colleagues who were registered in the names of their grandfathers or uncles.

In addition, in some marriages, although they are legal, the husbands leave their gypsy wives in their areas since their families undertake or swear that these wives won't engage in any of gypsy jobs. On their part, the husbands frequently visit their wives and spend on them and their children.

Table – 43- The survey of the research sample shows whether these marriages were successful or not.

Area	Yes	No	Total
Kamaliya	3	7	10
%	30	70	100
Fawwar	3	6	9
%	33	67	100

The success rate of these marriages appears close in the two areas, which is approximately one-third. We doubt the continuity of these marriages, as some such marriages did not last for long, and even if they lasted for ten years, as we know, the two parties separated. That is what happened in some marriages in Qadisiya Governorate. Meanwhile, such a marriage remains a stigma on the husband. Such marriage was prevalent among tribal groups in the area in the past. The sheikh at those times married a woman from his servants and called his son from her (the son of the maid or the slave). Similarly, the son of the gypsy woman is called (the son of the gypsy woman). The maid's son was not called the son of the sheikh to distinguish him from the son of the original wife, as they say.

Table 44- The place of residence of the gypsy wife of the non-gypsy husband in previous marriages.

Place / Area	Her family's house	Her husband's family house	Independent house outside the gypsy area	Independent house inside the gypsy area	Other	Total
Kamaliya	5	2	3	-	-	10
%	50	20	30	-	-	100
Fawwar	5	2	2	-	-	9
%	56	22	22	-	-	100

The above table shows that most of the gypsy wives live in their areas and within their families, and we explained the reasons for that.

Eighth: Neighbourhood:

Neighbourhoods serve as both physical spaces and social environments that shape how individuals and groups interact, build identities, and form networks of support. Here are the key aspects of the neighbourhood's role in social relations:

Queen and Carpenter define it as referring to an area where a group of individuals who know each other live and may exchange services and material things such as tools and equipment and generally do joint work. Ruth Glass defines it as a local group whose members meet for common motives throughout their area. They have their social contacts organised although they are spontaneous. Through the last two definitions, we note that the first one characterizes the area with the internal relations of its members, while the second deals with the local group and the common motives of its members that result from these relations. Both definitions agree that relationships are built on the basis and common motives of the parties of the relationship.

Here, in our study, we deal with the neighbourhood relationship that connects members of the gypsy community as a minority group with neighbouring non-gypsy groups and the nature of this relationship. It is not a condition that this relationship is good or based on a common interest, it may be an aversion, an antagonistic or a feud relationship... etc.

Neighbourhood relationship in Kamaliya:

We are referring here to the relations that exist between the gypsy residents of Kamaliya, who live in the neighbourhood no. (757) and a part of the neighbourhood no. (759), and the rest of Kamaliya non-gypsy residents, especially their close neighbours, regardless of the nature of the relations that existed between them.

It should be recalled that the residents of Kamaliya, who are non-gypsies or Arabs, as gypsies call them, are those who were displaced from (southern Iraq). Their number is about (20 thousand people) as estimated (in 1994). The end of the 1960s and 1970s were the peak of their displacement. The nature of the Kamaliya non-gypsy community (Kamaliya Arabs) is characterized by the following:

1. Most of them retain their tribal values, and this is clear through the presence of tribal sheikhs in the area and neighbourhood, neighbourhood kinship in housing and the presence of host halls of some sheikhs and notables. In addition, this is confirmed by the presence of titles based on tribal pedigree and the presence of pedigree schemes and trees for many of them.
2. They are Muslim Shia, most of whom are conservative and religiously committed, have established mosques and Husseiniyats, and are keen to adhere to religious events and rituals.
3. Some rural occupations still exist, including buffalo breeding, among some residents of Al-Fadiliya in the suburbs of the area.
4. Some strong ties and roots connect these residents with their relatives in their original areas.

Since we have learned about the nature of the professions practised by the gypsies and the charges and features attached to them, they will undoubtedly result in the following:

1. The conflict of values between Arabs and gypsies, as the practice of such acts as sex trade (sex work and brokering) and mirth (singing, dancing and music) and the consequences of these acts that contradict Arab values.

2. Religious conflict, as Islam rejects and prohibits such professions in general. God said in the Holy Quran: " Do not go near adultery. It is truly a shameful deed and an evil way.", He said "O you who have believed, indeed, intoxicants, gambling, [sacrificing on] stone alters [to other than Allah], and divining arrows are but defilement from the work of Satan, so avoid it that you may be successful. Satan only wants to cause you animosity and hatred through intoxicants and gambling and to divert you from the remembrance of Allah and prayer. So will you not desist?"

3. The presence of cultural and ethnic differentiation and a sense of high status.

4. The fear of the people of the area (Arabs) of their sons and daughters being corrupted and slipped into the sinful way by the influence of the gypsies.

5. Problems occur because of population convergence. There is a misunderstanding by some of the visitors to the gypsies and mistakenly go to the Arabs' homes, so problems occur. They also happen when Arabs' relatives come from other areas, going into the internal streets leading to their Arab relatives' homes, where they are exposed to problems of fraud.

6. The absence of patterns of known social relations among neighbours, affinity relationships, cooperation and others, not to mention the business relations between gypsies and shopkeepers.

The problems appeared as the following:
1. Arabs (non-gypsies) file several charges against gypsies, except for the practice of sex work and brokering in it, which we call (the sex trade). They file other charges against them, such as kidnapping girls (young or old) and trading with them (as white slaves), robbery crimes, fraud, and the spread of some venereal diseases, including HIV.
2. Most of the Arab residents of Kamaliya are ashamed to mention their real address. This happens especially while they are in the military service, being students and employees for fear of being accused of being gypsies, in order to avoid any problem in this regard. There have been incidents that demonstrate this (some gypsy soldiers from the area who were killed (martyred) in the war had inaccurate addresses. Some of their bodies have been identified through major addresses such as the Baghdad Al Jadida or Al Mashtal police stations or by local Mukhtars).
3. A few people living next to the gypsies sold their houses there to avoid suspicion, the houses were sold to gypsies or to people who rented them.
4. The difficulty of going through the internal sub-streets of this gypsy area due to incidents of fraud, and direct assault in various ways.

Arab residents' reactions in the area appeared as follows:
1. Hostile behaviour and severe prejudice by them against the gypsies. That manifested in anger and outrages such as beating some gypsies and, in another incident, one, carrying a rifle (machine gun), broke into the house of one of his gypsy neighbours, opened fire on the family, killed three of them and wounded a number of others. There are also many quarrels, and the two parties are intolerant of each other.

2. A Some Arab Mukhtars and notables from the area filed petitions and complaints to the minister of interior, the president and some members of the National Council (Parliament), and the Directorate of the Baghdad Al Jadida district, to the mayor of Rusafa district and to the party branches and organisations to find a solution to this problem. They propose to transfer the gypsies and deport them to any other place.
3. In 1993, the Ministry of the Interior, in response to the complaints of the Arab population, conducted raids in the area and gathered large numbers of gypsy men and women. They were punished by shaving their heads, arrested, and then returned.
4. Following this raid incident which was accompanied by a rumour that the government was displacing them from this area. Some Arab residents of the area went out to the streets cheering, rejoicing and congratulating each other. Delegations of them went to thank the official authorities such as the police station and the party organisation.

The gypsies' reactions were as follows:
1. They showed reservation and caution towards any aggressive behaviour against them by the Arabs, as they did not trust any stranger, and they avoided contact with their Arab neighbours.
2. They also showed evasive behaviour by writing the phrase (Arab's house), i.e. non-gypsies, on the walls of their houses or doors. That was in order to woo or deceive Arabs and police, when the latter tightened their control over their practices, to say that they were Arabs and have nothing to do with what gypsies do. But this phrase was interpreted as a code or a password for customers who visited them that they could find what they wanted in this house.

They may also replace this phrase with "house for sale" (see the economic pattern and sex trade chapter chapters).

3. They sought to consolidate their relationship, or as they claimed to do so, with some police officers or some officials to strengthen their position in this regard.

4. They showed some adaptive manifestations such as respecting (the sanctity of the month of Ashura) and stopping working on the tenth day of it.

Result:

From all this, we conclude that the nature of the neighbourhood relationship between gypsies and Arabs in Kamaliya is one of hostility, aversion, and prejudice on the part of the Arabs, and fear, caution, and an attempt to get out of a predicament on the part of the gypsies.

The credibility of this view and the result of our fieldwork study were confirmed after the fall of the previous regime and the chaos and insecurity aftermath. Some religious individuals in Kamaliya incited people against the gypsies. They raided their homes, robbed and looted some of their possessions and forced them to leave the area, despite the fact that the number of gypsies there was about 2000 people, under the pretext that they were " a hotbed for crime, drugs and sex work". Some accuse them that they had the protection of the pillars of Saddam's regime because they held parties, entertainment, and sex work for them... As soon as the gypsies were expelled, people demolished their houses, and took away doors, windows, and bricks, leaving piles of rusty rubble stretching for two kilometres... The gypsies have found another shelter now, they are staying in an old military complex, which was bombarded and destroyed during the war and lies a few kilometres far from their old place of residence.

And they spend sultry summer days in temporary huts with iron roofs or rooms without roofs. They get water from the public tap, while the electricity supply is intermittent at best, as it is currently happening all over Iraq". [167]

Neighbourhood relationship in Fawwar:

It is represented by the relationship between the gypsies in Fawwar and their closest Arab neighbours, who were the farmers living in the village of Al-Jamiyya, which lies (2 km) far north of the gypsy village. The road leading to the gypsy village passes a long Al Jameiyah village and through its farms. The gypsy village is directly bordered only by some farms which are a few hundred or tens of meters away.

This relationship is characterized by the following:
1. Since the inhabitants of the neighbouring village are farmers and maintain kinship relations among themselves, as most of them are from the Al Hamad tribe. They are a conservative society, which absolutely and completely rejects all these gypsy activities. However, they look at them with contempt and see the gypsy men as (procurer, sex work brokers) and the gypsy women as (adulteresses). They do not establish relations of affection, respect or affinity.
2. The closeness of the gypsies caused a problem that was always repeated, it is the problem when some people came to visit the gypsy area for the first time and mistakenly went to Al Jamiyya village misjudging that the villagers there were gypsies, and many quarrels occurred with those (gypsy customers). Therefore, these

---

[167] Ashsharq Al Awsat newspaper in London, 8-7-2003.

farmers carried a feeling of hatred and prejudice towards the gypsies, although it was less than the feeling, we found among the Arabs of Kamaliya because there was no direct contact with them since the gypsy village was isolated from them. They are more conservative and cohesive and there is no anonymity in their surroundings, so they are not afraid of the corruption of their sons and daughters, because it is not easy for a girl to go to the gypsy area exposed to the villagers, who are all considered as her family. The prevailing feeling here is regret for the gypsies' presence near them.

3. There were commercial transactions as some farmers in the village of Al Jamiyya sold some of their products to the gypsies.

4. The farmers had a positive sense of selfless and ethnicity, on the contrary, the gypsies had a negative feeling of inferiority.

Result:

The nature of the neighbourhood relationship between the gypsy community in Fawwar and the farmers, their neighbours, in Al Jamiyya village is one of avoidance of contact and caution.

Compared to what happened to the gypsies in Kamaliya by their neighbours after the fall of the regime and the deterioration of the security situation. Their counterparts in Fawwar did not get what happened in Kamaliya, and the avoidance relationship remained. But the caution of the gypsies in Fawwar increased and their previous activities decreased or even almost disappeared. In addition, many of them emigrated outside Iraq, especially those who have good financial capabilities or have artistic talents and other qualifications, specifically beautiful girls to work as dancers in nightclubs in some of Iraq's neighbouring countries such as Syria, Jordan and the UAE.

Some of them formed dance art teams that participated in the video clip works of Iraqi singers.

Gypsies' view of their reality:

Table 45 - The answer of the research sample to the question of whether they wish they were non-gypsies.

Area	Yes	No	Total
Kamaliya	47	7	54
%	87	13	100
Fawwar	41	5	46
%	89	11	100

The data of the above table shows that the gypsies' vast majority are dissatisfied with being gypsies, and they wish they were not, and we touched on that during the fieldwork study. When a gypsy speaks about himself or his community in front of someone who is not a gypsy or in front of an official or another notable person, he says, 'We are gypsies, concerning the listener' and this speech, which is sometimes said by the gypsies about themselves, is undoubtedly an admission of the inferiority of their social status.

It also shows the weak self-esteem of these people, which is an admission of rejection of their professions, and their prevailing status is undoubtedly the reason for that. It is also the result of the difficulties they encounter as a result of their collision with the wider society that rejects them.

This feeling and this situation will inevitably affect the construction of the

gypsy personality, which will arise weak, shaky, and negative. This will happen as well to the upbringing of their children, as many deviations will early emerge due to negligence and poor education.

Table 46 shows the extent to which the research sample prefers to change their professions.

Area	Yes	No	Total
Kamaliya	8	46	54
%	15	85	100
Fawwar	33	13	46
%	72	28	100

The data in this table shows a wide difference in the answers of the sample of Kamaliya's gypsy families from those of Fawwar's gypsies. In Kamaliya, area only (15%) preferred their lifestyle change compared to (72%) in Fawwar. This difference is due to the following:

1. Kamaliya gypsies are better off than others in the rest of the gypsy areas in Iraq, due to the availability of job opportunities for them in their location in Baghdad and the availability of services provided.

2. The importance of their location is represented in the value of what they own (for example, the high value of their houses because they are in Baghdad, the capital) and this can be applied to other properties they own.

3. Those who do not prefer to change their lifestyle are convinced that there is no suitable alternative solution better than the situation they are in.

4. This comes in contrast with the situation of the residents of the Fawwar gypsy area, who suffer from several things, including:
   a. The poor condition of their houses.
   b. The lack of provided services.
   c. Their location is relatively remote from cities; therefore, they bear high transportation costs.
5. This is in addition to the presence of relative religious and social influence, (adaptive) or due to the pressure of society and its rejection, and therefore they prefer to change their lifestyle.

We had to put forward alternative solutions to the current gypsies' lifestyle and in the survey of the study sample in the two studied areas, the responses were the following:

Table – 47 - What business do you prefer to practice in case your situation changes?

Works/ Area	Government jobs	agriculture	Trade	Artistic band	Work in a factory	Taxi driver	Other	Total
Kamaliya	-	-	3	3	-	2	-	8
%	-	-	37.5	37.5	-	25	-	100
Fawwar	2	14	3	2	4	7	1	33
%	6	42	9	6	12	21	2	100

It turned out that working in trade and artistic bands came first for Kamaliya gypsies who wanted to change careers, followed by taxi driving. The preference to work in a government profession is absent (perhaps because of its low wages and the gypsies' lack of skills). Similarly, the preference to work in a factory is also absent and in agriculture too because the gypsies used to live in cities.

As for Fawwar gypsies, the profession of agriculture came first (42%), followed by working as a taxi driver (21%), then working in a factory, trade work, government jobs, working in an artistic band and others, respectively.

The preference for agriculture appears in the first place because it is a simple job that does not require skills, and its financial incomes is big. As for car driving, it is desirable for them because of their urgent need for it as they suffer from transportation and its high costs.

Social adaptation conclusion:

The chapter on social adaptation can be summarized as follows:
1. The adaptation of the gypsies is characterized by matchmaking, as cultural features from the prevailing culture were adopted while retaining other cultural features. The result is that the gypsies in Iraq were distinguished by adaptation and uniqueness, and this is a gypsy feature known globally.
2. The adaptation was in two types, which are subjective (for gypsies) such as (religion, fashion, language, stability, meals patterns and others). The other type requires both parties to the relationship (Arabs – Gypsies) represented in friendship, neighbourhood, affinity, interaction, as well as the sense of national belongingness (citizenship) after acquiring Iraqi citizenship. This means at least a degree of social acceptance by the government and their feeling of being part of Iraqi society and working under that feeling. But this relationship is based on the material interest of both parties if it happens, and it does not express public satisfaction, especially by the Arabs.

3. The social adaptation here, according to the exchange theory, is the emergence or the appearance, which is the result of the interaction of the elements, created new features that were not inherent in the elements and unexpected in advance from their interaction in the light of the examination of the separate and independent elements themselves. These are also built based on taking material profit and loss into consideration and similar examples in all studied forms of adaptation.

4. Kamaliya gypsies are more adapted to the totalitarian society (the dominant culture), through their wider interaction with non-gypsies. This is due to the availability of opportunities for them more than other gypsies from other areas such as Fawwar, if we exclude the neighbourhood relations with the residents of neighbourhoods or houses close to them in Kamaliya. These relationships were characterized by Arabs' strong hostility or prejudice towards gypsies and gypsies' fear and caution.

Chapter Ten

The gypsy's conditions in Iraq now

The Gypsy's Major Problems in Iraq

The study's Findings

Recommendations to treat the gypsy's reality in Iraq

The gypsy's conditions in Iraq now

After the fall of the former regime in 2003, the conditions of the gypsies in Iraq worsened. They became the most vulnerable among its diverse groups due to the control of extremist religious parties and militias in various parts of the country and the typical stereotype of the gypsies there, derived from their practice of actions that are contrary to religion and social values. They were a "legitimate" target for these groups. It is difficult for small groups like the gypsies to protect themselves in such circumstances. They are a minority that is not used to organised and armed mass conflict, and they used to live with and under the protection of others. They are nomadic tribes living under the sheikhs' protection if they settle within the tribes' lands.

An example of what the gypsies were exposed to is their displacement from their area in Kamaliya in Baghdad. The displacement was caused by some irresponsible individuals of Kamaliya, after the political changes that took place in Iraq starting on April 9, 2005, because they (gypsies) were "a shelter for sex worker and religion-breakers, and that their presence in this conservative area is a source of constant discomfort and inconvenience to its people". The lawlessness that occurred after the fall of the former regime helped to carry out these unfair measures. Islamic values that encourage to follow a wise policy were not taken into account. They should have been given an initial warning, for example, to stop the previous practices that were considered as charges against them, and justifications to their forcible deportation from the area where they lived for decades. In addition, humanitarian values were not taken into consideration like excluding the olds and children from this collective punishment. Thus, they were displaced into ruins or former army camps in the suburbs of Baghdad.

We can affirm that the values and teachings of Islam require following gradual methods that begin with wisdom and good preaching and perhaps do not end with what those people started to do to the gypsies. In the 1990s of the twentieth century. When Imam Mohammad Sadiq Al-Sadr declared himself as a chief cleric in difficult circumstances. He appealed to the gypsies to give up their professions and ways of livelihood and lifestyle. He addressed them in the best way possible. [168] Many gypsies reacted positively, when a number of them offered their allegiance, despite they were under the protection of the former regime and did not need Al Sadr at that time. And supporting Al Sadr at that time was dangerous, as the regime tightened on him and monitored his movements and those who visited him. Both the offices of Al Sistani and Al Sadr even gave the gypsies promises not to be attacked, after what happened to them in their current crisis, to encourage them to return home. [169]

Many foreign parties tried to accuse the Islamic religion of being behind what happened in general and the Iraqi tolerance in particular, which was shaken after the recent political changes, and what the gypsies suffered from in Iraq is an example of it. An example of these foreign parties (in addition to the Arabic and foreign reports and articles cited here) is the article published on The Religion's homepage, entitled 'In now-religious Iraq, no tolerance for Gypsies' [170] which depicts the miserable situation of the Gypsies, which is difficult for any human being, as the lack of mercy and inhumanity threw these people without shelter, electricity, water, adequate housing, health

---

[168] Friday sermon no. 45

[169] The report of the Reuters news agency, which was published by Al-Zaman International Newspaper on January 5th, 2006.

[170] http://www.philly.com/mld/philly/news/11823843.htm . June 6th, 2005.

services and security protection. They took refuge in former army camps or took refuge with the foreign forces on Iraqi soil. That made them feel nostalgic for the days of Saddam Hussein and consider them more humane than those who followed him. Some of them sold their homes to their neighbours or the people of Kamaliya area, at a price ten times lower than the real price, according to their claim.

Some of the foreign forces in Iraq, including the Spanish forces that were present in the province of Qadisiya (Diwaniyah) in south-central Iraq, provided some kind of protection for the gypsies when they resorted to them and set up tents at the gates of the military base to seek protection after religious militias displaced them. In 2004, these forces returned them and provided some support, which compensated them for part of what they had lost and for the damage they had suffered. But after the withdrawal of these troops, their situation became worse than before.

The armed religious militias, especially the " Mahdi Army", are accused of using violence and violations against the gypsies. The website of American media website PBS reports that " in the last week of March 2004, Al Mahdi Army raided a small village inhabited by 1,000 - 1,500 gypsies, claiming that they were practising singing and dancing, razed their homes to the ground, killed a number of them, tortured and displaced others". [171]

---

[171] PBS Media Website, An Interview with prof. Dr. Adeed Dawisha, "Adeed Dawisha, is professor of political science at Miami University of Ohio -- he's written extensively on the politics of the Middle East". http://www.pbs.org/ newshour/bb/middle_east/jan-june04/turmoil_4-5.html

Humanitarian Affairs [172], stated, under the title "Gypsies call for greater rights", on March 3rd, 2005, that "in 2003, following the fall of the former regime, Al Mahdi Army militia attacked the homes of gypsies in Diwaniyah, cut off power supply and destroyed the only school in their village". [173]

These religious militias apply "provisions that they believe to be from the Sharia," such as flogging, head shaving, and others, against the gypsies and even their non-gypsy visitors are believed to come to their gypsy village in Fawwar.

It was reported that "a group of Al Mahdi Army detachments in Diwaniyah governorate arrested and punished everyone of –deviant- young people who go to the area of vice and corruption (gypsies) in front of other people. The number of deviants reached almost 100 of them on the first day of Eid al-Fitr. On the second day of Eid, the number of detainees reached 750 people in several governorates. Those detachments also arrested a number of drug and alcohol suppliers of non – Iraqi nationalities and handed them over to the police directorate in the province". [174]

It is also stated in the report of the United Nations Office for Humanitarian Affairs that the small village called (Al Zuhur) – a new name for the Gypsy village in Fawwar, which belongs to the province of Diwaniyah and located 180 km south of Baghdad, is a centre for gathering gypsies living in mud houses and tents. Their story

---

[172] It was noted that this report does not represent the opinion of the United Nations.
[173] Relief Web, http://www.reliefweb.int/rw/RWB.NSF/db900SID/DDAD-6A5NFE.
[174] Association website http://www.iraqirabita.org/index.php?do=article&id=2610
5-11-2005.

is too long to tell, as they suffer from poverty and difficult conditions such as a lack of health, social and educational assistance as well as power and water supplies and protection from religious movements that persecute them.

Their main sources of livelihood are singing and dancing, which they have been used to for hundreds of years, and they have not mastered other professions. Moreover, they are not educated, or not educated enough to get a job, and if there is an opportunity for getting a job, they will face racial discrimination as being gypsies.

On my last visit (December 2006-January 2007) to Iraq, I visited Diwaniyah so many times. I did not see any presence of militias or popular forces besieging the area at that time, except for the presence of a checkpoint of Iraqi security forces, at the beginning of the short road leading to the village, after things have been settled down. I recognized the fact that this Gypsy village, which became famous as "Fawwar", lives in almost complete isolation. Its visitors, who were constantly coming at old times, were not coming anymore. It means that their financial income was cut off, and the continuity of their lives became difficult.

Of course, they are included in the governmental food supply program as all Iraqis are, but many of their requirements, such as fuel, safe drinking water and their need to visit cities for medical, educational and other purposes, complicate their lives more and more. This pushed many of them to emigrate out of Iraq (Syria and Jordan in particular) and then to some Gulf countries or to seek asylum in Western countries. The rest of them are waiting for their turn to leave, through relatives and acquaintances who have arrived there.

As for the Gypsies in the Abu Ghraib area, which is located about 30 km west of Baghdad, the situation there is not better than it is in Kamaliya or Fawwar. Their sufferings are the same as the gypsies in Kamaliya area. The gypsies there claimed that members of the Zoubaa tribe, which forms most of the population in Abu Ghraib, attacked them with weapons and bombs and displaced 136 families which left their money and homes back, and moved to some former military barracks. One of those barracks is located on the Baghdad-Abu Ghraib Road, where there are more than 10 gypsy families living in rooms, each room shelters 9 gypsies. Zoubaa tribe members accused former president Saddam Hussein's regime of settling down the gypsies in their area to degrade them and tarnish their reputation because former President Abdul Salam Aref and his brother President Abdul Rahman are members of this tribe. Saddam had exempted the gypsies from the requirement of registration in the 1957 census, for the residents of Baghdad, and granted them the privilege of ownership and housing in the capital, like his cousins, while the people of this area and other Iraqis were deprived of this privilege. [175]

The situation of the communities of other villages is likely to be similar to what happened in these places mentioned here, due to the similar circumstances and the similar cultural structure of Iraqi society, although Reuters news agency report says that "the gypsies of the village of Hadid near Baquba may be the happiest among the gypsies of Iraq". [176] (i.e., what happened to them is less than what happened to others).

---

[175] Imam Al Laithi, the gypsies seek shelter after Saddam, Islam online website http://www.islamonline.net/Arabic/news/2003-05/06/article09.shtml on 6-5-2003.
[176] Ibid.

Despite the difficult conditions of the gypsies, the majority of them were keen to participate in the elections held on January 30, 1, 2005, as the nearest voting centre was located at a distance of 20 km away, as the report states. The report also adds that the photos of the former prime minister in the interim government (Dr Iyad Allawi) were present in most of the village houses because they thought that he was the most suitable and able to provide protection for them.

Many of them justify their participation in the elections by saying that they want a united, free, and democratic Iraq.

Now they hope that the government will offer some kind of protection and care to them, and they also do not hide their aspiration to emigrate outside the country, asking for mercy and humane treatment like the rest of the gypsies in the world. [177]

The surrounding society looks down on them because of their reputation. Some of the society demanded gypsies' deportation while others believed that they should have equal rights in the new Iraq.

It shows the disregard and negligence of the Iraqi people and civil society organisations, either because they were influenced by prevailing stereotypical ideas and judgments, or because they fear the power of radical religious movements. The Iraqi Red Crescent Organisation, according to its spokesman, said in a statement to the United Nations Integrated Regional Information Network (IRIN)," that they do not know what is happening to the gypsies, and that the organisation did

---

[177] Ibid

not provide them with any support or assistance due to the lack of sufficient information about them?"!! [178]

The local government in Diwaniyah provided the gypsies with some limited services as being Iraqi citizens, just like others, and therefore they should be included in any social development plan, says a member of the Municipal Council in the province.

Many gypsies, especially dancers and musicians, emigrated to neighbouring countries, specifically Syria, Jordan, and the Gulf countries, where many settled in Dubai because of its entertainment venues that give them opportunities to keep in touch with their talents and skills and offer them financial income. With many former Iraqi cabaret artists, gypsies form artistic groups that present their art in the theatres of these countries. There are accusations that a number of them are involved in sex work in these countries.

The gypsy areas' Problems:

The fieldwork study that we conducted in the Kamaliya gypsy area in Baghdad, and Fawwar in Qadisiya governorate, was to see the social adaptation of the gypsies and compare the adaptation of the two models of gypsy housing in Iraq.

In Kamaliya, the gypsies' houses were close to non-gypsies' houses whereas the gypsies' houses in Fawwar were isolated representing an isolated housing model (ghetto) which is like other gypsy areas in Iraq.

---

[178] Ibid

The first type of the gypsies' housing in Kamaliya caused several problems, among them are:

1. The problem of the constant collision between the gypsies and their Arab neighbours (non-gypsies), and this collision was represented in a hostile conflict and severe prejudice shown by the Arabs, especially against the gypsies, because they consider gypsies as violators to (religion, traditions and law) because of their professions. That led to the emergence of a counter behaviour on the side of the gypsies in the form of so-called ethnocentrism, extreme conservation, and constant fear of attacks, and we mentioned some of those in this study. As we witnessed, the situation evolved to the point that the attack on the gypsies and displacing them from their homes became, in the eyes of some, a legitimate matter, and all that happened in the absence of responsibility and law that protects them.

2. The closeness in housing may attract and spoil the sons and daughters of their neighbours (non-gypsies) due to friction, imitation, and temptations.

3. Some non-gypsies commit shameful acts and crimes and attach them to the gypsies.

4. Some gypsies, or some who claimed to be, caused fraud problems.

The second gypsies' type of settlement, which is prevalent in Iraq, whose model is the Fawwar area, which we studied, has the following problems:

1. The gypsies suffer greatly from the lack of services provided for them and the negligence that affects them:

   a. Most gypsy areas suffer from a lack of access to safe drinking water, forcing them to bear the costs of buying water at exorbitant prices.

b. These communities are far from the cities and most of them face a lack of paving roads to those cities, which leads to exorbitant transport costs.

c. Their areas' internal streets are not paved.

d. No food agencies are allowed in the gypsies' areas that are linked to the distant city centres.

e. There is a lack of close schools in most gypsy communities, therefore, their children did not join or drop out of school.

f. Health service is absent, as there are no health centres in their areas, except for periodic health teams although some of them were not sincere in doing their job. Furthermore, most gypsies evade examination by these teams, because, being representatives of the government, they may know about their diseases. They prefer to visit private clinics instead and this decision is up to the gypsy him/herself, and this is difficult due to his/her poor awareness and difficult financial conditions.

The gypsy areas are the most dangerous as being a hotbed of epidemics and infection. It is feared that the spread of dangerous venereal diseases, including the deadly aids.

i. The police are absent, which means the presence of a lot of violations and crimes. And even if the police are present on some occasions or situations, some of them are dishonest and they abuse the honour of the profession in exceeding or cruelty to them, even with non-gypsies.

j. They used to earn easy money and such a lifestyle.

k. They have no skills, competencies or scientific degrees that enable them to work in other fields.

l. The community rejects them and identifies them wherever they may be.

m. There is no easy and ready alternative solution.

The Study's Findings:

In this study, we addressed the topic of social adaptation of the gypsies in Iraq, and we started the study with an introduction about gypsies. We used the theory of social exchange by George Homans, Peter Blau, Thibault and Kelley as a theoretical framework for the study.

The results of the study were the following:

1. The gypsies form a subculture within the culture of the wider Iraqi society (the dominant culture). They are different due to their cultural, professional and value differentiation through their practices of professions that contradict the prevailing culture of religion and law. That exposed them to social ostracism. Therefore, they can be called a (cross-cultural).

2. The gypsies form an ethnic minority whose origins belong to Indian tribes that migrated to the region and the world in the form of tribal waves and took many names.

3. Kawliya, as a name, was derived from the name of King Kawl in India, where these tribes lived, and their women served in the temple of King Kawl. This is evidenced by the nature of the work that some of their women did, such as singing, dancing and sex work, for the priests and pleasure seekers, for money. They were called (servants of God), and these actions are like the gypsies' actions practised today. It is believed that after their migration they felt honoured to carry the name (Kawliya).

4. The increase in the size of the gypsy family, especially in the Kamaliya area, a single family there had (10.3) members whereas

the family in Fawwar had (9) members, and this accumulation is due to reasons including:

a. The difficulty for the family to divide due to the high costs of buying or building a house. Although the income of the gypsies is high, they have too many requirements and they spend a lot, especially on fun, gambling, makeup...etc.

b. The nature of the gypsy profession requires many people in the family, to protect the family from the aggression of some customers or win any quarrel with a stranger, or the purpose of forming an artistic band.

c. Gypsies share residence with some relatives, or some non-gypsy who live with gypsy families, especially sex workers or gypsies' employees.

5. Illiteracy is at a high level among the gypsy household's heads, as gypsy children early drop out of school. That leads to almost complete cultural illiteracy besides alphabet illiteracy.

6. Kinship and marriage systems are similar among gypsies in Iraq along with what is prevalent in Iraqi society. It is a manifestation of social adaptation.

7. The complex and residence sharing family is the predominant model.

8. Marriage age among gypsies is delayed, as most of the study sample agreed that the ideal age for marriage, for both genders, is limited to the age group (21-25) years. Among the reasons behind delaying the age of marriage, as the study sample believes, is the rise of dowries, as the dowry of some girls, especially very beautiful ones, reaches almost imaginary figures, such as a quarter of a million, one hundred and fifty thousand or two hundred thousand dinars, because the girl is an important source

of income for the family. Moreover, most young people can satisfy their sexual desires in the area.

9. The gypsies follow the Islamic religion, which is an adaptive manifestation of the wider society because the official and dominant religion are Islam.

10. Gypsies in Iraq generally follow Islam and they know that their professions and most of their actions are contrary to the Islamic religion.

11. The gypsies of the Fawwar area are closer to religion than the gypsies of Kamaliya, due to their location in a relatively conservative society as well as being closer to the holy places in Najaf, Karbala and Kufa. Nevertheless, Kamaliya is in Baghdad, the capital, where there are fewer holy places nearby.

12. The main professions of the gypsies are: (singing, music and dancing), sex trade (sex work and brokering in it) and commercial business (owning and managing stores and shops selling alcoholic beverages).

13. Most of the professions of gypsies are undesirable and even rejected by Iraqi society.

14. The economy of the gypsy family depends mainly on women, and the more daughters the gypsy has, the wealthier he will be.

15. The main gypsy crafts are dangerous and anxious for them, they depend on general circumstances, and they are not productive, rather they are consuming, serving and recreational.

16. The biggest deterrent and affective controlling factor on the gypsies is the power of law represented by the police, while religion comes next, with a huge difference, then the tribe and tradition come last.

17. There are no clear controls and interest in children's upbringing and education, due to the nature of life, as the professions they practice are reflected in it.

18. The Fawwar gypsy area has the advantage of being more compliant with social control factors than the Kamaliya area. This reflects a kind of adaptation in this aspect.

19. All communication tools are available for the gypsies with the wider community, and the Kamaliya area has the best luck in this due to its location in Baghdad, which offers this opportunity.

20. Social adaptation is characterized by matchmaking, as some cultural features are replaced by the features of the dominant culture while retaining other features, and that grants them the characteristic of adaptation and influence.

21. There are two types of social adaptation here: self-adaptation, represented by (fashion, religion, language, stability, and some cultural manifestations such as making food, etc). The second type of adaptation requires honesty and cooperation from both sides of the relationship (gypsies and Arabs) and is represented by affinity, friendship, neighbourhood, and direct interaction relationships such as buying and selling ... etc. These relationships were false and based on the interest of both parties to the relationship, which is very little, and like a bubble, quickly fades. Although the gypsies seem ready for the relationship, the other side constantly refuses relationships, such as the neighbourhood relationship between gypsies and Arabs (non-gypsies) in Kamaliya.

The gypsies are ready to adapt easily and integrate into society, but they are not ready to leave their professions easily for several reasons that we mentioned earlier.

22. Kamaliya gypsies are generally more adaptable than Fawwar gypsies in most aspects of their lives due to their constant contact

with the wider society if we exclude the tense neighbourhood relationship with their Arab neighbours. This relationship is characterized by prejudice and extreme intolerance against them (which did not turn into violence). That's due to the gypsies' professions and actions which are in contrast with the culture of the wider society in general and the nature of this (neighbouring) society which is relatively conservative due to its tribal roots and its religious obligations.

23. The research hypotheses were realized as follows:

    d. The second hypothesis, which is (that the profession of parents has a significant impact on the upbringing of their children), was realized after studying the economic activities and professions practised by the gypsies and the accompanying negative impact of these professions on the educating and upbringing of their children.

    e. The third hypothesis of the research, if the subculture is characterized by some values that clash with the norms of the wider society. This exposes it is exposed to rejection and social ostracism) was realized.

    f. The fourth hypothesis of the research: (the process of social interaction leads to adaptation) was realized. This is done by reviewing the means of communication and interaction that the gypsies have with the wider community to achieve some kind of adaptation.

    g. The fifth hypothesis of the research: (social relations strengthen and deepen if the profits for both parties are equal to the costs and become weak by the imbalance between the relationship and its profits) was realized. This was done through the study of marriage (affinity) relations with non-gypsies and friendship relations, which were purely material based on profit.

24. Gypsies are ready to adapt easily and integrate into society, but they are not ready to leave their professions easily for several reasons that we mentioned earlier.

Recommendations to address the reality of the gypsies in Iraq:

Below are the following proposals for the concerned entities. We hope that they will be up to the level of the studied problem:

1. It is important to recognize, first and foremost, that not all gypsies are deviant or outside the bounds of religion, tradition, and law. They are a community that has inherited an array of customs, traditions, and experiences, and they have also faced various pressures and challenges shaped by their life circumstances. There are innocent children in this society who are imbued with the culture in which they grew up. " A man's mind only grows within the limits of the template that his society makes for him". [179]

Most gypsies, like drug addicts, need treatment, not punishment, and that is why we put forward the following suggestions:

- To provide adequate security protection for the gypsies in all areas of Iraq, in accordance with religious and humanitarian values that protect the vulnerable, children, the elderly and women, and to

---

[179] Al-Wardi, Ali, the farce of the human mind, Al Rabita press, Baghdad, 1955, P.172.

avoid collective and arbitrary punishment by unauthorized people and entities.

- To gather all the gypsies in Iraq in one area, and offer jobs that are suitable for their competence, for example, agricultural land, since agriculture does not require great skills.
- To provide them with educational, health, administrative and consulting services. All these services should be subject to a higher central authority, and their cadres should be changed from time to time so as not to cause administrative corruption or nepotism in dealing with gypsies.
- Tightening full control over those who repeat previous bad actions.
- To nurture artistic talents and organise them in a modern way.
- To promote education for the gypsy children, for both genders, for all stages and in the long term, by providing facilities for the gypsy children, as the following:

a. To offer close schools.

b. To exempt them from some financial obligations that are sometimes required of students.

c. To provide school supplies of stationery and others, at regular intervals throughout the school year.

d. To grant financial and moral rewards to the gypsy children in general and those who excel among them in particular.

e. To exempt them from the average requirement for admission to some Iraqi institutes and colleges (especially Fine Arts) to encourage them to continue studying and education, and this is a system followed by some European countries such as Bulgaria. [180]

---

[180] This was reported to the author by Dr Majeed Arif.

References:

Al Ani, Muzahim, Communication and its role in the social change, doctoral thesis in Greek (not published) introduced to <u>Pandious</u> Greek University, 1992.

Al Bayyati, Aladdin, Ilmulijtimaa Bein Alnadhariya wal Tatbiq, Dar Attarbiya, Baghdad, 1975.

Al Hassan, Ihsan, Problems of Inter-Marriage and Mixed Families, Al-Taliya House, Beirut, 1994.

Al Nouri, Qais, Subcultures and the Problematic Professional Development in the Arabian Gulf, Journal of Arab Studies, Issue 4, year 29, January - February 1993.

Al Ruaishidi, Saadi Faidhi, Introduction to Anthropology, Higher Educations Presses, Mosul, 1989.

Al Ruaishidi, Saadi, Anthropology of The Arab Homeland, High Education Presses, Mosul, 1990.

Al-Far, Ali Islam, Dictionary of Sociology, 1st edition, Egyptian Encyclopaedia, El Maarif House, Egypt, 1978.

Al-Hadithi, Taha Hamadi, Gypsy and Qarach in Iraq, printed by Mosul University, 1979.

Ali, Younis Hammadi, Introduction to Demography, University of Mosul, 1985.

Al-Khashab, Ahmed, Social Control: Its Foundations and Practice, Cairo Bookshop, 1968.

Al-Nouri, Qais, Iraqi rural woman's participation in domestic decision – making, Journal of Comparative Family Studies, vol. XXIV, No. 1, 1993.

Al-Nouri, Qais, The Family as a Development Project, Cultural Affairs Press, Baghdad, 1994.

Al-Qashtini, Khalid, The Forgotten Holocaust, an article published in The Middle East newspaper in London, issue No. 8229, June 9th, 2001.

Al-Samarrai, Mutaib and Al-Hashimi, Hamied, The Impact of Mid-State Characteristics on Social Behaviour, a paper presented at the first conference of the Faculty of Arts, Qadisiya University, 1994.

Alyan, Rushdi and Samouk, Saadoun, Religions: A Comparative Historical Study, Ministry of Higher Education Press, Baghdad, 1976.

Arif, Majeed Hameed, Cultures and Peoples, Al-Kutub Publishing House, Baghdad, 1993.

Arif, Majeed, The Anthropology of Communication, Dar Al-Hikma, Baghdad, 1990.

Beals, Ralph & Hoger, Harry, Introduction to General Anthropology, Vol.1, translated by Mahmoud Al Jawhari, Al Nahdha Press, Cairo, 1965.

Dinken, Michelle, Dictionary of Sociology, translated by Ihsan Al-Hassan, Dar Al-Rashid, Baghdad, 1980.

Diwaniyah Mayor Office, with editor Mr. Fahim on April 30th, 1994.

Duncan, Mitchell, Dictionary of Sociology, translated by Ihsan al-Hassan, Al-Rashid Press, Baghdad, 1980.

Durant, Will, The Story of Civilisation: Our Heritage, part 3, Vul. 1, Simon & Schuster, New York, 1942.

Franser, Angus, De Zigeuners, Atlas-Contact, 1st edition, 1999.

Greenfield, Howard. Gypsies, Crown Publishers. Inc. New York, 1977.

Grolier, Encyclopaedia, vol. 10, Distributed by the Grolier Incorp Orated, New York, 1961.

Hanna, Nabeel Subhi, Gypsy Groups with a Special Reference to the Gypsies in Egypt and Arab Countries, 1st edition, Al-Maarif publishing house, Egypt, 1980.

Hassan, Ali, Baghdadi Al-Turath Al-Shaabi magazine, vol.2, in 1-18 September 1968.

Ismail, Farooq, Social Relationships Among Ethnic groups, 3rd edition, Qatari Ben Al Fuja'a publishing house, Qatar 1986.

Jawad, Mustafa, Gypsies in Arab Resources, Al-Arabi magazine, Kuwait, issue no. 126, May 1969

Jean-Paul Clebert, Gypsies: A Historical and Folklore study, Translated by Lutfi Al-Khuri, Cultural Affairs House, Baghdad, 1976.

Mahjoub, Mohamed Abdou, An Introduction to the Socio-anthropological Direction, The Egyptian Book Organisation, Alexandria, 1977.

Mair, Lucy, Introduction to Social Anthropology, translated by Shakir Salim, Al Hurriah Press, Baghdad, 1983.

Manchip J. White, Anthropology, English Universities press, London, 1954.

New Webster Dictionary.

Notice the United Nations Universal Declaration of Human Rights issued on 1-12-1948, Al-Maaref Press, Baghdad.

Palmore, Hirsch & Ariffin, International Communication and the Diffusion of Family Planning in West Malaysia- Demography

Publication of the Population on Association of America, vol. 8, No. 3, August 1971.

Rashid, Fawzi, Who Are the Gypsies, a study under publication, College of Art – Baghdad University, 1994.

Roney, Horacio, The wild tribes of India, B. R. Publishing, Cooperation, Delhi, 1974.

Sugarman, Barry, Sociology: theory and consumption, translated by Mohammed Al-Gharib Abdul-Kareem, 5th edition, the Universal Office, Egypt, 1988.

The Directorate of Nationality Affairs, Qadisiya Governorate Branch, a pamphlet that includes a conclusion about the gypsy, and it is internally circulated.

The Encyclopaedia Americana, International Education, vol. 13, New York, 1976.

Webster's Third New International Dictionary, vol. 1, A.G.

Al-Wardi, Ali, the farce of the human mind, Al Rabita press, Baghdad, 1955.

Young, Gay, Gender Inequalities and Industrial Development, Journal of comparative family studies, vol. XXIV, No. 1, spring 1993.

Zeitlin, Irving, The Contemporary Theory of Sociology, translated by Mahmoud Oda and Ibrahim Othman, printed by Thatulsalasil press, Kuwait, 1986.

Newspapers & websites:

Al-Zaman International Newspaper.

Association website http://www.iraqirabita.org/index. php?do=article&id=2610 5-11-2005.

Imam, Nahla, Gypsy Issue Throughout History, Al-Safeer Lebanon Newspaper, 6-6-2000.

Imam Al Laithi, the gypsies seek shelter after Saddam, Islam online website http://www.islamonline.net/Arabic/news/2003-05/06/ article09.shtml on 6-5-2003.

Iranian Al-Wifaq Newspaper, The Historians of the Holocaust and exaggeration in numbers, no. 2274, March 11th, 2004.

Mansoor, Nadia, Gypsies in Egypt, Al-Shabab Magazine Egypt, 1989.

PBS Media Website, An Interview with prof. Dr. Adeed Dawisha: http://www.pbs.org/newshour/bb/middle_east/jan-june04/turmoil_4-5. html.

http://www.philly.com/mld/philly/news/11823843.htm . June 6th, 2005.

Rajko, Djuric, Gypsies' Journey Throughout History, Al-Arabi Kuwaiti Magazine, Vol. 364, March 1964.

Relief Web, http://www.reliefweb.int/rw/RWB.NSF/db900SID/ DDAD-6A5NFE

Sheikh Ali, Khalil, A Stop on Kawliya Ways, Al-Balad newspaper of Baghdad, issue (353), July 9th, 1965.

Ashsharq Al Awsat newspaper in London, 8-7-2003.

Al-Shabab TV, Baghdad, 9pm news of April 22nd, 1993.

Baghdadi Arab World Newspaper, Baghdad, issue no. 3977 on Aug. 22nd, 1937.

El-Messiri, Abdel-Wahab, Jews, Judaism and Zionism, Nazi extermination against gypsies, Gypsies Nazi Extermination of ‹ http://www.elmessiri.com/Zionism/jewish/ENCYCLOPID/ START/..%5CMG2%5CGZ4%5CBA4%5CMD1111.HTM‹ 11-3-2007.

Facts about Germany web site, http://www.tatsachen-ueber-deutschland. de/ar/history/content/glossary03.html?type=1&tx_a21glossa-ry%5Buid%5D=1467&tx_a21glossary%5Bback%5D=151&-cHash=e2cc4b7507.

Wikipedia Free Encyclopaedia on the Internet, ar.wikipedia.org, March 10th, 2007.

Fonisca, Isabel, Gypsies' Biography, a conclusion review published in Al Zawraa web site: http://www.alzawraa.net/home/index. php?option=com_content&task=view&id=6902&Itemid=232‹ 10-3-2007.

www.ingramcontent.com/pod-product-compliance
Lightning Source LLC
Chambersburg PA
CBHW051243020426

42333CB00025B/3032